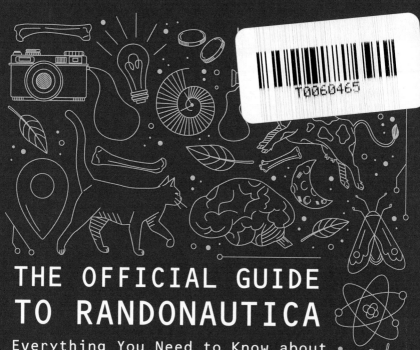

THE OFFICIAL GUIDE TO RANDONAUTICA

Everything You Need to Know about
Creating Your Random Adventure Story

Joshua Lengfelder and Auburn Salcedo
Founders of Randonautica

ADAMS MEDIA

NEW YORK   LONDON   TORONTO   SYDNEY   NEW DELHI

Adams Media
An Imprint of Simon & Schuster, Inc.
100 Technology Center Drive
Stoughton, Massachusetts 02072

Copyright © 2021 by Joshua Lengfelder and Auburn Salcedo.

All rights reserved, including the right to reproduce this book or portions thereof in any form whatsoever. For information address Adams Media Subsidiary Rights Department, 1230 Avenue of the Americas, New York, NY 10020.

First Adams Media trade paperback edition July 2021

ADAMS MEDIA and colophon are trademarks of Simon & Schuster.

For information about special discounts for bulk purchases, please contact Simon & Schuster Special Sales at 1-866-506-1949 or business@simonandschuster.com.

The Simon & Schuster Speakers Bureau can bring authors to your live event. For more information or to book an event contact the Simon & Schuster Speakers Bureau at 1-866-248-3049 or visit our website at www.simonspeakers.com.

Interior design by Colleen Cunningham
Interior illustrations by Alaya Howard
Interior images © Getty Images/ulimi, Barmaleeva

Manufactured in the United States of America

1 2021

Library of Congress Cataloging-in-Publication Data
Names: Lengfelder, Joshua, author. | Salcedo, Auburn, author.
Title: The official guide to Randonautica / Joshua Lengfelder and Auburn Salcedo.
Description: First Adams Media trade paperback edition. | Stoughton, MA: Adams Media, 2021.
Identifiers: LCCN 2021005922 | ISBN 9781507216255 (pb) | ISBN 9781507216262 (ebook)
Subjects: LCSH: Randonautica (Mobile app) | Digital maps. | Orientation. | Voyages and travels. | Chance. | Chaotic synchronization. | Travel writing.
Classification: LCC GA139 .L46 2021 | DDC 796.58--dc23
LC record available at https://lccn.loc.gov/2021005922

ISBN 978-1-5072-1625-5
ISBN 978-1-5072-1626-2 (ebook)

Many of the designations used by manufacturers and sellers to distinguish their products are claimed as trademarks. Where those designations appear in this book and Simon & Schuster, Inc., was aware of a trademark claim, the designations have been printed with initial capital letters.

This book is intended as general information only, and should not be used to diagnose or treat any health condition. In light of the complex, individual, and specific nature of health problems, this book is not intended to replace professional medical advice. The ideas, procedures, and suggestions in this book are intended to supplement, not replace, the advice of a trained medical professional. Consult your physician before adopting any of the suggestions in this book, as well as about any condition that may require diagnosis or medical attention. The author and publisher disclaim any liability arising directly or indirectly from the use of this book.

Certain sections of this book deal with activities that may result in serious bodily harm or even death. The authors, Adams Media, and Simon & Schuster, Inc. do not accept liability for any injury, loss, legal consequence, or incidental or consequential damage incurred by reliance on the information or advice provided in this book. The information in this book is for entertainment purposes only.

Contents

Part 1. Randonautica ... 13

Chapter 1. The Origin Story ... 15

Chapter 2. The Spirituality Behind It All ... 40

Chapter 3. Theories and Beliefs on Consciousness ... 57

Chapter 4. Understanding the Science of Randonauting ... 73

Chapter 5. Connecting to the World ... 97

Chapter 6. Getting Started ... 125

Part 2. The Adventure Log ... 145

Preface

by Auburn Salcedo

Have you ever met someone, looked them in the eyes, and felt like you've known them forever? The sensation of familiarity is unshakable. A long day of waiting led up to a moment where I felt that experience of knowingness when I met my now partner and dear friend and the coauthor of this book, Joshua Lengfelder, for the first time. Josh was traveling from Dallas to see me in Orlando in December of 2019 for, well, we weren't really sure. We just knew we needed to meet in person. I had found Josh, better known by his alias "Comrade," after stumbling across a mysterious fringe subreddit of curious, kind, and sincere explorers of the unknown, the Randonauts. I was immediately intrigued, and somewhere in me I knew I'd play a larger role in helping this radically new community move into the mainstream eye.

My first message to Josh was quite cryptic: "Hello, I am not sure how I am supposed to help but I just have this gut feeling I needed to reach out to you." Josh was always quite accommodating to my weirdness. I could tell he'd spoken to many people unsure of their purpose within the community. After a bunch of somewhat vague conversations, Josh spontaneously took a flight to Orlando—a flight that was supposed to arrive at 10 a.m. but turned into an 11 p.m. arrival after several delays.

I pulled up to the airport, found Josh waiting, waved ecstatically, got out of my car (nearly before I had fully parked), and ran over to receive a greeting with the biggest, friendliest hug. For just a brief second, I wholly felt the sensation that I'd both known him forever and I'd know him forever. Once we got in the car, it was like we'd been friends for ages. He explained the value of breaking free from daily routine. I shared how I had been posing the question "When was the last time you did something random?" to myself and others. I prodded him with many questions about the theories behind Randonautica, and then I sought out an answer to something that had left me dumbfounded. I told him my story of the orange traffic cone.

Back in July of 2019, I made my first Randonaut trip. The point from the bot that was used at the time landed me on an orange traffic cone. Well, that's not too surprising; I was on a busy road. On my next stop, another orange traffic cone, at a construction site. Living in Omaha, Nebraska, makes traveling from an urban setting to the country just a quick fifteen-minute drive, so I headed toward the more rural area to generate another set of random coordinates to travel to. The coordinates led me to a cornfield. I walked through the stalks, pretty freaked out, honestly. Even though I grew up in the Cornhusker State, there is still this eeriness about walking through a cornfield when you're 5 feet, 3 inches and can't see above the head of the corn maze. I trudged forward, committed to making it to the "You've arrived at your destination" moment from my GPS, and moments before I did, I stood in shock. Wouldn't you know it? Right there, probably 200 feet into this cornfield, was **an orange traffic cone.**

I asked Josh, "How is this possible? That there would be an orange cone in the middle of the field. This doesn't feel random." He posed many different theories (which we'll discuss later in this book). Josh and I made three Randonaut trips while we were together the next day. The first brought us to a lone, little orange cone, like the ones you'd see in a PE class. We both squealed and laughed. My conscious awareness was heightened, and the thrill of the unknown journey was coursing through me. The second stop brought us to a point on the side of the highway, which I thought was a bust. But Josh jumped out, walked straight to the area, moved some dead grass—and hello! Another orange cone! Last, we ended up at a manufacturing lot where, at first, we saw nothing of importance...but then, in between 30-foot-high white packing containers lining the lot, there on its side lay one lonely orange cone. I looked at Josh and said, "C'mon, did that just fall from the sky?!" We laughed.

It's an odd sensation to have a feeling of total uncertainty with no idea where a journey may take you, when right and left turns seem completely out of your control. You start to realize something magical happens when you go back to a childlike state of wandering with wonder. From my first trip to my current adventures, the impact of breaking free from my routine and being somewhere for the sake of randomness has changed my life and worldview forever.

Random voyages by way of the Randonautica app have allowed me—as well as over eighteen million people around the world—to break outside of our mundane realities and begin to play, seek, and find through randomness with our local environments. I've had experiences that are hard to explain, coincidences that seem impossible, and most importantly, a lot of fun.

From mind-bending encounters to eye-opening landscapes and legendary scavenger finds, stepping into the unknown is showing there is more to the world than we ever thought possible.

Introduction

When was the last time you did something random? Actually, it might be easier to start by listing the things you do that *aren't* random at all. For instance, I bet you brushed your teeth this morning. (If not today, yesterday you did, right...right?) You probably showered recently and put clothes on. If you work, perhaps you got in your car and drove the normal route you always take. You likely ate a selection of food you've had before made with ingredients or packaged goods from the grocery store you always shop at, or you ordered from a restaurant you've frequented in the past. Whatever your routine is, it's part of a series of habits you've created over time.

We Randonauts like to call this your "probability tunnel." Your probability tunnel makes it crazy hard for you to make random decisions and break out of your own personal matrix. Ponder for a moment how you came to be reading this book. Was it a sequence of events that planted your eyes to this text or simply a coincidence? Think about not just where or how you acquired this book, but why. Then go back as far as you can from that moment, further and further.

Let's assume there were an infinite number of small occurrences that had to happen in order for you to be in this precise time and space. What role did you consciously play? What if every move you've made—emotional responses, left turns, right turns, choices in relationships, your work, your hobbies, the media you've consumed, and all your other habits—has been part of a predetermined order of your life? In other words, your probability tunnel. A long, narrow, enclosed path that you follow aimlessly day-to-day. How can you escape it? You're basically operating like a human algorithm.

All right, maybe that's a lot to imagine at this point. However, you'll be pleasantly surprised to learn how adding a random event to your life path—which you can find via the Randonautica app—can take things off course in a positive way and wake you up to the world around you that exists outside of your conscious awareness.

You'll join a vast community of other Randonauts all around the world who are finding that there is something more to this app than the randomly generated coordinates. Like so many others, you may find that the intention you set in your head while using the app could influence what you find at the location.

In this book we'll explore the theories behind why Randonauts are encountering both personally meaningful coincidences and synchronicities as well as patterns that match what others have found, and also the science, spirituality, and mind-bending ideas that all add up to the global phenomenon that is the app Randonautica. You'll also be able to record your Randonaut trips in the journaling pages, tracking your travels, intentions, and observations. Capturing the details of your trips, your feelings about and reactions to the journeys, and notes about symbolism and meaning on the journal pages can help you notice overarching themes. For instance, you might find over the course of twenty trips, more than half involved something that had to do with animals, even if that wasn't your original intention. This could lead you to a better self-realization about your love for animals and wanting to volunteer in an animal shelter, adopt a pet, or (like one Randonaut) change your course of study from accounting to becoming a veterinarian!

Let Randonautica and this book work hand in hand to help you break out of your probability tunnel, visit new places, test the limits of your consciousness, and find adventure all around you.

PART 1

RANDONAUTICA 101

The story of Randonautica is the story of millions of people reaching out into the world, searching for novelty, and relating it back to themselves in the form of significance and meaning. After all, novelty is something that can inspire you in your daily life. It is something abrupt that changes the way you view the world and adds a little spice to an otherwise routine existence. Randonautica also uses mind-matter interaction technology, which offers the challenging change in worldview that your mind is more connected to the material world than most may suspect at first glance.

Get ready for a wild adventure as you learn about the project from its founders' perspective and get an inside look at the phenomenon that has infused novelty into millions of people's lives. You'll learn about the science, various theories, and spirituality behind the app and how you can join in the fun.

CHAPTER 1

The Origin Story

Randonautica, the mysterious viral sensation that took the world by storm during the global pandemic in 2020, has become something of an urban legend. But what are the truth and the motivations behind the project? In this chapter, you will learn the intentions and inspiration behind the app and also get a brief look at the early days of the project and even some pre-Randonautica history. You will get the inside scoop from the creators themselves and get to see the initial motivations for the app that eventually took the world by storm.

What Is Randonautica?

Randonautica is a way for people of all different ages and lifestyles to generate a truly random point to adventure to. Understanding what Randonautica *is* can be better achieved by first establishing what it is *not*. For starters, you will come to learn in this book that Randonautica is not a normal app. Randonautica is not simply one thing. It's not a game or a navigation resource. It's not just entertainment or a social media tool. Randonautica broke the mold on how people interact with technology, their own awareness, and the environment by stepping outside the bounds of what people believed a mobile app could do.

Randonautica, or being a "Randonaut," can bring about a new way of seeing and feeling the world. From its foundational theory to its practical application of traveling to unknown places, Randonautica is riddled with mystery and depth that are beyond the scope of a boxed-in explanation. Randonautica is also built from varying theories, many of which you will learn in this book. Because of this, in many ways, Randonautica is the first of its kind.

Even further, some people would suggest that to wholly understand what Randonautica is, you first need to experience using it. That the sensations and realizations cannot be explained with words. How an individual perceives their first Randonaut journey will vary greatly depending on a tremendous number of factors, including their age, lifestyle, past circumstances, cultural background, and belief systems; the environment they are venturing into; their mode of transportation; even how the weather is that day! Randonauting is about *you*. If you are reading this and haven't taken the first step outside your probability tunnel, it is the hope of this book that you can gain a greater knowledge of Randonautica so you feel comfortable and eager to do so.

TERMS TO KNOW

Probability tunnel: an abstract representation of the idea that limited decision-making possibilities based on a human's previous experiences and patterns create a likely "probable" response.

The more mysterious aspect—and the conundrum of the question "What is Randonautica?"—lies in this: What do *you* believe Randonautica is?

The First Randonaut

What type of person would have the drive to spearhead a community of wanderers of the random? Directing people into randomness and being there to help empower them through the sometimes life-changing experience is not a volunteer job the average person would necessarily sign up for. However, for Joshua Lengfelder, it was almost meant to be. Josh's life story is filled with examples of him looking beyond traditional ideas and finding enchantment in places others see as normal.

Eventually, Josh began to personally test the bounds of a laissez-faire approach to life, letting the random take over. In college, for instance, he chose his major by picking one randomly from a list and landed on electronic media and communication. During his studies, Josh became interested in how groups form and grow. He dreamed of creating a grassroots storytelling platform capable of crossing cultural boundaries on a global scale.

This research led Josh to the field of memetics, or the study of how ideas are transmitted virally. One day, Josh set out looking to find a treasure within the digital landscape—something that he'd have to fall into an Internet rabbit hole to uncover. He soon stumbled across a channel on Telegram, a global messaging app, discussing theories and sharing knowledge pertaining to the memetics field. The world of memetics is actually composed of a very small, selective pool of researchers. Josh was surprised to have found other minds that he could discuss ideas with at great length, and he became enthralled with theories of human connectivity. Josh also became deeply interested in the concept of treasure, and determining where tangible and intangible hidden gems in life might be found.

TERMS TO KNOW

Randomness: unpredictability; the quality or state of being without a pattern or framework of organization.

It wasn't long before Josh, known then by his handle "Comrade," was introduced to a handful of anonymous "mad scientists" who called themselves the Fatum Project (the word *fatum* is Latin for "fate" or "destiny" and refers to a deterministic fate and its byproducts). They began sharing the details of their experiments and confiding in Josh that although they had been working on their research for years, they feared it may never be able to be used by the public due to the oppressive country they lived in. The Fatum Project was created underground, and its creators had to stay anonymous due to strict laws of their country.

As soon as the Fatum Project creators shared with Josh their research on going to random places, it was like fates had collided, and Josh knew what he had found was treasure. The concept of sending people to random places was innovative, and it had never really

Early Experiments with Randomness: Situationists' Walks

The first iterations of testing how to send people to random places were set in urban locations and were highly based on Guy Debord's Theory of the *Dérive*. In the late 1950s, well before Randonautica was created, people had been going on random walks to change their routines and get alternative glimpses at their realities. *Dérive*, which translates to "drifting," is basically a random walk. The people who went on these random walks were called "Situationists." Among other things, the Situationists were trying to break out of their normal frames of reference of an urban layout and instead treat the varied ambiances in the landscape like a playground, walking wherever their unconscious minds told them to go and disregarding the normal routine flow of the city in favor of more interesting and playful approaches. They would do things like walk in a straight line through a dense urban environment, instead of being guided by normal routine such as going to a park or getting a coffee or visiting a friend. The idea was to reshape how people view cities and to develop a more holistic perspective on the urban environment as a living, breathing creature.

The *dérive* was useful for disrupting the normal flow of routine and gaining a different perspective, but the locations the Situationists explored were never *truly* random; they were simply guided by a different sort of human awareness than that of most people walking through a city.

been done before on a large scale, but with Josh's flair for showmanship (which, fun fact, he learned while working as a roustabout and performer at Lone Star Circus in Dallas, Texas), he knew he would be able to make this incredible technology accessible to the entire world. The Fatum Project members decided to make a plan to collaborate together and create the greatest mind-matter interaction experiment the world had ever seen.

The Fatum Project took the Situationists' concept one step further by asking: What if the walk included a destination? Well, that is exactly what happened in one especially important early Randonautica experiment, in which seventy thousand participants were sent a set of randomly generated coordinates in their urban setting, with no reason or explanation for why they were sent the coordinates. These locations were generated with pseudorandomness (you will learn in Chapter 4 why that matters). After the locations were sent out, some interesting, unexpected things started to happen.

Many participants went to the random locations and noted different types of existential experiences:

- One woman went to the coordinates in the middle of the night and was taken to an empty highway road. As she walked in the middle of the road, she experienced a sort of unity of consciousness, as if her mind had been linked to an inexplicable intelligent force. (This was not the last time someone would report a mind-unifying experience while visiting random locations, but it is important to the history of the Randonauts because it was the first time someone had such an experience at a location, and it set the stage for more experiments to come.)
- One of the random coordinates ended up being under a highway, where the participants found *another* set of coordinates graffitied on a highway pillar.

- One of the strangest phenomena associated with this experiment was that even years after the coordinates were sent, people were visiting the locations and experiencing strange things. The events didn't seem to be limited by time, leading to suspicion of a possible retrocausal event, something in the future influencing the past.

The compelling information gleaned from this experiment meant one thing: People welcomed the opportunity to test the idea of random travel in an easy way in their own lives.

The Beginning of the Movement

Once word started to spread that odd things happen when you travel to random coordinates, a small group of people quickly centralized. They started escaping their regularity and opening their minds to the idea that something more existed outside of their perceivable realities. The Randonauts subreddit on *Reddit* had an influx in users across the globe sharing stories, inviting others, and becoming Randonauts. The word "Randonaut" is a portmanteau of "random" and "nautical," meaning "randomness explorer," and the Randonauts' stories were not only mind-bending but oftentimes connected. People were also corroborating similar feelings like despair or fear on their first time out.

Others were telling stories of odd occurrences, like coming across people who appeared to be out of place—for example, a woman seemingly inexplicably staring into the distance while standing still, or a man walking in circles around a small fence. People weren't the only ones acting strange; animals were overly friendly and approachable. Cats, dogs, birds, even larger animals like cows and horses would gently mosey their way over to the stranger stepping into their otherwise predictable animal world.

People also started to realize that there appeared to be an invisible connection weaving one Randonaut to the next. How was it possible that several people, none of whom knew one another, were posting similar stories, experiences, findings, and feelings? People were befuddled, posting comments like "I don't understand how there are so many posts with photos and videos of multiple black cats just sitting in random places! How are you guys finding these herds of black cats?!" One thing was for certain: What was happening was sensational, bewildering, and about to take the Internet by storm.

Then, one day, owls started to appear. It seemed like every Randonaut at that point (a small group of maybe three hundred people) started seeing owls on their trips. Shortly after, one of the Randonautica developers (also known as "devs") realized he actually had placed an owl statue on top of the computer server that all the random points were being requested from! He had found a strange antique owl while Randonauting and had absentmindedly placed it on the server. During the time the owl statue was on the server, people started seeing owls. Weird coincidence? The Randonautica devs decided to experiment with this idea a bit more. They started placing objects on the server and waiting to see if they showed up in people's trip reports, and they did!

The first test was a regular container of salt. It took a few months, but someone eventually did report finding salt randomly at one of

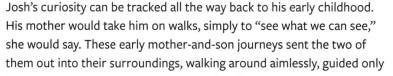

Randonauts' Adventures

Josh's curiosity can be tracked all the way back to his early childhood. His mother would take him on walks, simply to "see what we can see," she would say. These early mother-and-son journeys sent the two of them out into their surroundings, walking around aimlessly, guided only by their intuition. Josh took this habit of joyful wandering and held on to it, applying it to his lifestyle in his adult years.

their points. Next, they got a meteorite and placed it on the server in the hopes that participants would see UFOs, and sure enough, three people reported seeing UFOs at random points during the time the meteorite was sitting on top of the server. One Randonaut even got a pyramid-shaped UFO on video and posted it to the community!

A Growing Randonaut Community

As you can see, the journey to the Randonautica app began with eye-opening synchronicities, statistically improbable coincidences, and over-the-top finds that led to the discovery of something much bigger than originally imagined. As soon as Josh released the original version of Randonautica into the world, it was like a portal had been opened. People started finding connections they never would have before, realizing new possibilities, and making choices they wouldn't have previously conceived. As the community grew, the stories became laced with deeper oddities. Photos and videos started to accompany wild legends that some had tried to debunk. In spite of their differing stances on certain finds, a group of growing enthusiasts began to learn and spread the ways of the Randonauts.

Much speculation began to take effect as people in and outside of the community considered how these common and bizarre occurrences were continuing to happen among such a broad range of people. The early group of users had a number of highly speculative theories about what could be taking place with this newfound technology. For example:

- A "simulation theory" group believed the hypothesis that all of reality, including the earth and the rest of the universe, was an artificial simulation built or run by AI, similar to a computer game like *The Sims*. They claimed that by

Randonauting, you'd break the matrix, the simulation that your character was supposed to follow.

- Others thought the only explanation was chaos magic and occultism, that the app was releasing information that had belonged to esoteric societies for hundreds of years.
- Some people started rumors that Josh was a member of the Illuminati, or that he was a powerful reptilian alien.
- Still others believed an external force was involved, that the app was a clear line to a higher power or instant manifestation.

Many more ideas unfolded and were greatly debated. Most of these theories arose from a basic misunderstanding of what Randonautica was trying to achieve. Randonautica isn't supposed to break you out of "the matrix," like in the movie. It isn't about whether the world is real or fake. It *is* about breaking out of the complex web of probabilities that keep an individual stuck within a particular frame of perspective of reality. Lots of people would make the mistake of assuming some higher power or personified force is keeping people within stasis, but it is just a pattern, one that is easily broken by adding a small amount of randomness to your normal routine.

The forums, social media platforms, and chat lobbies continued to expand, attracting many hobbyists to the early project. The people who occupied the Randonauts dev room came from a variety of backgrounds and fields, including:

- Quantum physics
- Engineering
- Hardware/software development
- Academic research
- Statistics and data science
- Parapsychology

The group would toggle from 15–30 people at any given time, and all participated in ways big and small to help the efforts to further understand, share publicly, and even attempt to prove the phenomenon that was unfolding with the Randonauts. Whether they were interested in hacking away at the code or true believers in the concept, wanting to offer their talents, the collective effort of great minds was a launching pad for what would come next.

However, this lively group was challenged with two things:

1. Many people didn't understand what was happening in the Randonauting process, and thus they were tasked with trying to explain dense theory.
2. The program was not user friendly, because it was simply a bot within a messaging app (more on that next).

The growth of the community meant there needed to be advancements in how to reliably generate truly random coordinates and how to make them accessible to the public.

From Beta Bot to Randonautica

These developers were using Randonautica in its most primitive form, when it was known as the "shangrila_bot" found through the global messaging app Telegram. The bot ran on a server from Josh's home computer and was similar to what you experience when you chat with a customer service "representative" that's not a human but instead is loaded with predetermined responses. The shangrila_bot operated the same way, but instead of getting responses like "Sure, I can help you with that!" you'd get the message "Choose quantum type." The bot would go through a series of prompts. Finally, you'd type "/getpoint" and the bot would run a quantum coordinate and output it for you to travel to. That was all it did.

Though it was simple, it took several steps and lots of instructions for newcomers to understand how to get access to and fully operate the bot. The pressure to create a stable, scalable, and sustainable way to have a Randonaut experience was growing. At this point, Josh was working not only on building up and supporting the community but also helping to wrangle together great minds to assist in the growth. He would post "help needed" requests in dedicated chat lobbies and on social media, and talented people stepped up to help create what would be the first Randonautica mainstream prototype.

The website bot.randonauts.com acted similarly to the shangrila_bot but was able to serve the needs of more users using higher bandwidth than what was available on the personal computer at Josh's house. The site had a Star Trek–meets–Indiana Jones feel and an underground, dark web vibe to it. In fact, many users thought that it was from the dark web! It was mysterious and different and took a lot more effort to use than a traditional app, which was sort of the appeal (for those people who could figure out how to use it!).

The web bot, known as the "beta" test of Randonautica, was quickly ported from a web page to be viewable on an app, and by February 22, 2020, the beta app was out and accessible to users all over the world. Once the word started to spread, especially on social media platforms like *TikTok*, *Twitter*, and *YouTube*, people flocked to the bizarre new way to adventure.

Going Viral

Many first-time Randonautica users will share one of three experiences: "I can't believe it worked, but it worked"; "I don't know how it worked, but it worked"; and "It didn't work." Users' belief or disbelief in the app's ability to provide extraordinary outcomes didn't matter—odd things were happening whether you expected them to or not.

Trending

In the blink of an eye, #randonautchallenge was trending globally. It was the summer of 2020, and in a bittersweet way, it was as if the universe had aligned the app's release just prior to the COVID-19 pandemic lockdowns and quarantine initiatives. People of every culture, nationality, age, and lifestyle were looking for activities they could do that didn't involve group interactions and outings in busy places. People were stir-crazy, and Randonautica offered a way to safely get out of the house and into nature for an adventure unlike any other.

#randonautchallenge became a lockdown trend, and more than one hundred million Randonaut trips were made in the spring and summer of 2020. There were so many people using the app that it was getting bogged down and crashing. Newbie Randonauts and "veterans" alike waited in line for downtime when fewer people were on the app so they could generate coordinates and step out of confinement and into the fun. In the meantime, fans kept binge-watching the stories being recorded, and the love for viewing unexpected journeys grew and grew. People quickly began to create platforms dedicated to Randonauting, including *YouTube* channels, *Discord* chat rooms, *Twitter* accounts, and even a reality show called *Ready or Randonaut*, which followed Randonauts on their first experience with the app.

Skeptics' Views

Of course, where there are believers, there are also skeptics. Many people seek ways to dismiss that there is anything special about Randonautica other than a random walk. One claim is that people's experiences are reflective of the Baader-Meinhof phenomenon, the idea that after learning something new or putting attention to something, you suddenly notice that word, concept, or thing everywhere. An example of the Baader-Meinhof phenomenon would be going to a car dealership and deciding that you like a certain vehicle because it's unique. You think about how you rarely see it, and so you begin to contemplate purchasing it. Then, in the following days, you notice the same make, model, and even color everywhere you go! Parked, passing by, in front of you at a stoplight. You wonder, *Did I not see this before, or am I only paying attention to it now because I am interested in the car?*

Another claim that skeptics use is confirmation bias, which is a tendency to give more favor and credence to information that confirms one's prior beliefs or values, causing people to interpret abstract information as evidence of their existing belief. An example of confirmation bias is believing that people who are left-handed tend to be more creative. While a person may not wholly believe this in the forefront of their mind, upon discovering someone is left-handed, the person could unconsciously only take notice of actions or qualities that affirm the left-handed individual has creative abilities. This type of confirmation bias is an easy way to describe the "you believe what you want" mentality and is certainly an oversimplification of the mystery of Randonautica. Still, skeptics do often take on Randonaut adventures to test mind-matter interaction, and skeptic-turned-believer reports are common!

The Suitcase

Now for the story you've been waiting for: the unfortunate incident of the suitcase. With millions of Randonaut trips happening all over the world, there were bound to be some real oddities uncovered...but no one expected what was found by a group of Randonauts on Alki Beach in Seattle. The Randonauts had set their intention to "travel," and near their point, they stumbled across several suitcases that had washed up on the shore. In true #randonautchallenge fashion, they recorded the entire experience on *TikTok*, and revealed an astonished young woman opening a suitcase to a stench. Realizing that the suitcases might contain something more ominous, the group called the police. It was later determined that there were human remains in the suitcases. After the bodies were identified, several weeks later a mystery was solved, and a family had closure for their missing loved ones.

The video made global news. Every outlet under the sun reached out to Auburn and Josh for comment, often trying to sensationalize Randonautica as a nefarious app. Diligent reporters would research and note in their stories that other adventure apps, like Pokémon GO, had also led to users finding human remains. Ultimately, finding a dead body is at least one in one hundred million for the Randonauts—clearly an anomaly! Still, the interest in, and mystery of, the app skyrocketed.

Randonautica Is Born

A rush of newbies downloaded the app to try it out. These rookie Randonauts, many of whom did not have a strong grasp on the underlying mechanism of Randonautica, brought many challenges. Mainstream users expressed confusion about the how and why, sometimes finding themselves having existential crises after trips that impacted their perception of reality. It was clear that the current version of the beta bot still wasn't fulfilling the educational needs of the users or the massive increase in traffic—which meant a full-release app needed to be created, and fast.

Improving the app required a lot of time and effort. Being a totally unfunded group came with pros and cons. The positive side was that the small team had lots of creative liberties. There were no investor milestones that needed to be met, and most importantly, the Randonauts knew they weren't being taken advantage of by some evil corporation. The challenges were obvious: building a company and quickly creating a scalable app to support more than eighteen million downloads. But we were up for the tasks that needed to be done—like letting the creative side thrive *while* organizing and creating structure for a previously decentralized group working in different places around the world. But in order for the app to be sustainable, there needed to be a plan in place.

Then there were the tedious steps that had to happen at a rapid pace to turn into an official company. We worked with lawyers, accountants, and customer support experts to establish product management infrastructures. We hired new developers to create a version of the app that would be sustainable in the long term. Finally, in September and October of 2020, the full-release Randonautica became available on Apple and Android.

The app is still evolving, and we have ongoing plans to create features that will empower the user to experiment with using Randonautica as a tool to enhance novelty in their life while experimenting with the possibility that the mind and the emotional output of a human being can have an effect on the matter around them.

Why Go Randonauting?

It's clear that millions of people use this app—what exactly draws them to it? The reasons people go Randonauting run the gamut from complete boredom to heightening their dimensional consciousness. The "why" is highly specific to each individual, but we have found some common threads.

Just for Fun

Oh, the excitement of being a child: carefree and able to find thrill in even the most boring of environments. There's just something about a random journey that ignites this same sensation. Roaming into the vastness of the world around you can spark pure enjoyment!

Randonauting can turn your locale into a playground of sorts. You can take a break from boredom and the daily grind and just explore, guided by complete randomness. Countless Randonauts have reported bliss and glee from the simplest things found in even their own neighborhoods. Randonautica makes walks more delightful, hikes more interesting, and group outings a blast. There have also been couples, new and old, who have used Randonautica to add character to their date nights! Randonautica and chill, anyone?

Of course, what "fun" means to one person can be very different from what another person thinks. While one person might enjoy frolicking in the newfound daisy fields Randonautica landed them in, another might chase the thrill of a heart-pounding night crawl into the dark woods. (Those interested in the paranormal often find their fun in a bit of a spookier fashion, such as seeking out areas like cemeteries.)

Randonauting with Friends

The most-viewed videos of Randonauting often simply highlight a group of friends shrieking and laughing in a car, in the woods, or in a landscape as mundane as a field. Thousands of self-recorded Randonaut trips show the hilarity of the mind unraveling and ideas expanding in a group setting—like a video of four young women peering out the car windows, excitedly shouting to one another, "I've *never* seen this before! *No way!*" as they make connections with what they're seeing. Imagine being filled with genuine excitement about otherwise mundane things like billboards, fruit stands, and bumper stickers....That's what can be fun about Randonauting!

To Enhance Your Spirituality

Randonautica is an amazing foundational tool for finding deeper meaning in your life. Regular Randonaut trips will encourage a growth in awareness and an ability to recognize and analyze patterns. Randonauts who set spiritual intentions often report an empowering sensation of having control over their destiny, or in some cases, having their fate shown to them by a higher power.

Various faith traditions share a commonality in describing steps to spirituality—states described as awakening, enlightenment, or nirvana. In several practices, especially in Eastern religions, the path to enlightenment is in large part attained by the individual breaking down their ego and connecting with their true self. Traditional

Randonauts' Adventures

One Randonaut explained their spiritual journey using the app as follows:

"I had grown up Baptist but found that I was questioning a lot of my religious beliefs. Not my faith in God, necessarily, but in the way I seemed to be engaging my spirit. For a while, I was almost convinced I was living in a *Sims* game. An immense need to explore something more came over me. I ended up in an Internet rabbit hole, and long story short, I met the Randonauts.

"My first trip, I was led to a small Buddha statue in the front yard of a house. It wasn't the Buddha that struck me. I stood there, realizing that I had remembered every moment of the trip. The turns I took, the little girl I had seen walking with her mom on the route, several billboard signs—it was as if I had photographic memory. I felt incredibly connected. I felt aware. I felt alive.

"After my first trip, I began setting intentions, like 'assistance with my purpose in life' and 'God's guidance' or 'a sign from the universe.' By my third day Randonauting, I started to weave together a pattern: seeing my grandmother's name and educational facilities in many places. Even when I wasn't Randonauting, I would find the pattern carrying into my daily life. I heard my grandmother's name during a discussion of people behind me in line at the grocery store. I started getting college and trade school pamphlets in the mail. I was in awe of how quickly I had changed from dread of the past and anxiety of the future to being right here, right now. I began to be filled with this intense sense of gratitude for God, the universe, and myself."

meditative practices include quieting the mind, and being present can help with this journey toward self-discovery.

How can Randonautica help you connect with your true self, you ask? While Randonautica does not require you to sit in lotus pose in a dark room, it does encourage mindfulness and self-awareness. Many of us live on autopilot, but Randonautica shakes you out of that perpetual state, bringing your focus to the here and now. When you visit someplace intentionally, you are more inclined to look around carefully and enjoy where you are.

Going on adventures also helps you notice patterns and symbols from the world around you. You might also become more aware of certain numbers, such as times (11:11, 2:22, 3:33, etc.) or dates.

One of the defining characteristics of the spirituality behind Randonautica is that it puts you in the driver's seat of your spiritual experience. There is no high priest or guru in the middle, no codified index of knowledge you must refer to. All you need is the desire to explore random locations, read the signs around you, and experience whatever may come.

Exploring Mind-Matter Interaction

Some people are drawn to Randonautica because of how it pushes the boundaries of commonly held beliefs about how human consciousness interfaces with the physical world. The idea that your mind is distinctly separate from the physical world is called "Cartesian dualism." Randonautica seeks to utterly destroy this concept by asserting that your intention is causative, and that by focusing your conscious intention and influencing some initial conditions, you can create vast differences in the trajectory of outcomes. These effects are probabilistic, which means they won't happen *every* time, but by focusing your conscious intent and using Randonautica, you greatly increase the chances of your intention manifesting.

What this means on a basic level is that Randonautica can guide you to places you were thinking about or talking about when you generated the point. The idea is that there is a relationship among intention, personal feelings, and personal significance that influences the random process. That's why you'll find yourself taken to places that are eerily connected to your internal state, a reflection of the internal in the external world.

These experiences range from extremely vague and subtle to completely overt and obvious, like going to a random place and finding a piece of paper with your first name on it. Mind-matter interaction creates order out of what is supposed to be totally pattern-less and random.

TERMS TO KNOW

Mind-matter interaction (MMI): a theory that consciousness and matter interact with each other in all forms, and particularly that intention can impact material reality.

Getting Off the Screens and Into the World

In an environment where daily active users, total time viewed, and clicks determine the success of a social media platform, Randonautica offers a different approach. By relying on the real world for content, rather than algorithmically filtered information bubbles, Randonautica opens you up to learning about things you never would have known existed. In fact, one of the early decisions about Randonautica was to make sure that as the app grows in functionality, the target will always remain to encourage people to go out and explore. Although other games and apps strive to find hooks and addictive tactics to keep you glued, Randonautica is the opposite. If you really think about it, the reason that Randonautica exists is to break you out of patterns. Patterns form from consistent programming, information, environments, and what makes up your daily mental diet. Randonautica is the anti-screen.

Because of how advanced entertainment and information sharing have become, it can be difficult to get off the "wake, eat, work, entertainment" treadmill. After mixing up your routine with Randonautica, however, it is not uncommon to lose interest in a once-favorite episodic

TV series, video game, or social media app. Instead, you start engaging more frequently and actively with *your own life*. Connections become easier to make, and it's as if you become an active participant in your life, instead of just blindly following your regular routines. Finding your own storyline takes you out of escapism and into a potently fluid reality.

How to Use the App

Now that you know a bit about how the app got off the ground and why people often use it, let's dive into actually getting started. We'll explain the nuts and bolts of what the app does, and also talk about how to apply yourself to the experience.

The Main Function of the App

On a basic level, Randonautica generates random coordinates and you follow them. Easy enough! You can dictate just how far you are willing to extend your journey to by setting your radius, the circle of distance around your current or a set location. Perhaps you want to take a short walk; in that case, you might want to set your radius to under a mile. Driving gives you more flexibility to set farther distances. Where you're headed is going to be completely random, but how far you have to travel to get there and what medium you use to travel—by foot, bike, car, or spaceship—that's up to you. Consider the weather conditions in the area and your means to reach this destination prior to setting your radius and venturing out.

Applying Yourself to the Experience via Intentions and Attractors/Voids

Even the experience of creating your settings is an element of choosing to embark on a Randonaut journey. You might be wondering why. How is this different from just throwing a dart at a map of your area?

There are two main reasons why using the app is more than just a random walk in the park, and they involve you as an individual. The elements that make this just as much about you as it is about the app are as follows:

1. You setting an intention for your adventure
2. The way you direct the app to choose your location—via "attractors" and "voids"

Let's look at each in more detail.

SETTING AN INTENTION

Randonauts sometimes ask, "Where do I set my intention?" as if there is a place within the app to type it in. Well, there isn't. As you set out for adventure, the theme for the trip only needs to exist within your mind. You set your intention by clearing your mind and having a strong idea of what you'd like to discover or have your trip guided by. All you have to do is give your intention some good thought as you're preparing for your journey and let Randonautica do the rest. Your intention can be as specific (say, "find a red door") or as open-ended (say, "seeking an answer to a life issue") as you like, but the stronger, clearer, and more focused you are with your intention, the more likely you are to observe things that are aligned.

This method has been used in various fields over the past several decades. For instance, in sports psychology, athletes are encouraged to "visualize" winning and set an intention (such as, "I'm going to be the champion") as a way to deepen a belief within themselves on a subconscious level. You can use this same technique with Randonautica. For instance, if you set your intention as "something that reminds me of my grandmother," you can visualize arriving at your Randonautica-delivered coordinates and being astonished at what you've found and how closely it aligns with a childhood memory pertaining to your grandmother. Or, if your intention is "I want to find money," you can imagine the feeling of money and the excitement of finding it, and even take it a step further and get into the thought of spending it! If you're seeking something broad, such as a feeling, you don't have to fill in the details, but you might imagine physical manifestations of this feeling—for example, how happiness gives you a warm glow or how excitement makes your heart beat quickly.

Whatever your intention, it helps to conjure deep feelings of emotional resonance. What this means is that you really experience the feeling of whatever your intention is. Try to see the process of setting an intention and generating a point like an extension of yourself, peeking into your higher mind and allowing a version of yourself to help you out by choosing a particularly interesting geographic location for you to visit that is perfectly attuned to be meaningful to you. Imagine that a version of yourself who is not constrained by time and space like a normal human, and has access to information you cannot normally conceive of, is aiding you in this process.

ATTRACTORS AND VOIDS

The second way you can impact how you interact with the app is by selecting whether you want an attractor point or a void point. To understand what those are, let's talk a little bit about the location points that Randonautica generates.

Randonautica uses a special algorithm to generate random points all across your set radius. Some of the points end up close together in a dense area (attractors) and some are spread out (voids). We refer to these areas as "anomalies." Anomalies are things that deviate from what is typical, standard, or expected. To understand this on the scale of real life, anomalies are events that are beyond coincidental and make you take a step back, almost dumbfounded as to how they could have occurred. In math, an anomaly is something that deviates to the point where scientists might say something like "Wait a sec, *that* shouldn't be there." This is the particular thing that Randonautica looks for in its two sources of anomalies.

Attractors, points in the dense area, are often described as locations of "high energy," but that's not necessarily the case. Understanding how randomness operates and also how an attractor can be found requires some imagination. Think of a 5-foot-long, 5-inch-diameter clear PVC pipe. The PVC pipe is standing upright and will act as the "tunnel" in this scenario. Poking through holes along the pipe are hundreds of tubes, like the small tubes at the dentist office that suck the spit out of your mouth. These tubes are blowing air at different forces and unpredictable intervals. This creates a tunnel of inconsistent airflow patterns. Now, let's say a large handful of salt gets poured into the pipe from the top of the tunnel opening. The salt will travel down the tunnel, being stirred and unpredictably disrupted by the blow tubes, and will ultimately land within the 5-inch circle at the bottom. When the tunnel is removed, there is a 5-inch circle of salt that remains.

TERMS TO KNOW

Anomaly: a deviation from the expected, normal order of things.
Algorithm: a set procedure to be followed for performing calculations or solving other problems, especially by a computer.

Now imagine looking at this circle of salt, how scattered and inconsistent it should be—patternless, a mess. What the mathematical computation that derives an attractor does is look for the anomaly in the salt. It says, "Whoa, wait, there is a *mound* of salt here! This shouldn't have happened. It should be chaotically distributed." Alternate to the attractor is the void. It's where the algorithm finds the least amount of salt. "Well, look what we have here, a segment with no salt at all!"

To relate this back to how the Randonautica app operates, the salt granules represent the coordinates, the tunnel is the generator, and the air is creating the entropy, or randomness. The Randonautica secret algorithm, known as the Newton Library, is assessing *your* circle, set as the radius on your map, and looking for the weirdest, most statistically improbable way the "salt" overlaid itself. Essentially, the app goes through an intricate mathematical process to get your pinpoint on your GPS. It's a mysterious-yet-scientific way of finding locations that are hopefully ultra-special in some way to you and the area around you.

You select within the app whether you want to go to an attractor point or a void point. Which one you choose is totally up to you. Here are some general thoughts about each one:

- Some people think that void spots are more eerie and airy and really have the feeling of being void of energy. There have been reports of voids having a higher despair rate or an uneasy feeling. But then other people say that they like voids for all sorts of positive reasons.
- Attractor points, on the other hand, have been known to have a denser feeling and bring Randonauts to places with lots of things to observe.

These observations could all be confirmation bias, of course, as the words "attractor" and "void" have strong connotations. Regardless, they are two different types of trips, and you can experiment for yourself with the effect of each type on your Randonauting adventures.

WHAT YOU'VE LEARNED IN THIS CHAPTER

- Josh created the Randonauts after meeting a group of "mad scientists" focused around the field of memetics.

- Randonautica started as a primitive bot in a messenger app and evolved into the full-blown app you see today.

- Part of the fun of Randonautica is having your own pet theory for how it all works.

- During the 2020 global pandemic, millions of people discovered Randonauting as a safe, socially distant activity, and Randonautica blew up as a movement.

- People Randonaut for fun, to enhance spirituality, and to explore mind-matter interaction.

- Setting your intention doesn't take place in the app; you set your intention in your mind.

- Attractors and voids are different types of anomalies Randonautica generates.

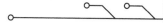

CHAPTER 2

The Spirituality Behind It All

Throughout history, people have been drawn toward deeper mysteries around them. Whether you are a curious seeker on the path to wisdom, someone hoping for spiritual growth, or a nature lover looking for meaning in the world around you, Randonautica can support your journey. Randonautica encourages you to find truth, explore your inner self, and connect with nature by exploring the environmental landscape. Many Randonauts have the sneaking suspicion that the world is not as it seems—that beyond the material realm there is some element of connectedness among all things and that by tapping in to this guiding force of coherence, one can perceive more of holistic reality.

This desire to see beyond the material world is not something new. Religions, cultures, and various traditions throughout all of history have tried to explain this external unknown and its relationship with humans and nature. Human beings have always felt that there is more to life than what we can simply perceive with our senses, and that with the right means, we can see beyond the normal limits of space and time. Because of this, different tools and methods have been developed over time to break us out of the confines of normal human knowledge, from lucid dreaming to divination to the relationship with God or a source. This chapter will look at a few of the influences from ancient and modern spiritual and religious practices that have similarities to those performed while Randonauting.

Synchronicity and Waking-Dream Space

When you start Randonauting, you begin paying closer attention and noticing things you did not before. Exploring unknown geographic locations increases your frame of perspective and allows you to enter new dimensions of possibilities. That which was hidden comes into view. The unknown location randomly generated by an avid Randonaut is not sterile or insignificant; instead it is teeming with life and meaning. By paying attention to synchronicities, or coincidences that are personally significant, you are entering into a sort of waking-dream space. The logic of synchronicities is like that of a dream: things connected by how they relate to one another. When you start paying attention and reading the signs and symbols, you enter a state that can be compared to a lucid dream.

The great goal of the alchemists of old was the transmutation of base elements (such as mercury) into gold. While engaging with this chemical work, there was also an inner work taking place for the alchemist. This might have looked like an inner transformation from their undeveloped self (like the base chemicals themselves) toward refining their spirit or creating a spiritually mature emotional nature (like the alchemical gold). Similarly, when the brave Randonaut ventures forth into the unknown to explore physical geographic locations, at the same time, an inner work of transformation is taking place. For the Randonaut, the alchemical gold is the process of inner transformation that occurs when you begin paying attention and start noticing blind spots in your perceptual frame of reference.

This path of transformation will not look the same for every person. Each individual has a unique ability to communicate with the universe, and the knowledge and understanding that come from that exchange will often seem cryptic and unintelligible to others who have not experienced it. Like explaining a dream you had to someone, you may be able to get some of the story across, but most likely you will not be able to truly communicate the experience in the way it happened to you.

Don't worry if you are unable to exactly convey the nature of your synchronous experiences to other people, especially non-Randonauts. Documenting even your own synchronicities, with their ephemeral and fleeting nature, is a challenging task. That's why the journaling pages in this book are so important. Keeping a consistent log of your experiences in Part 2 of this book, as well as writing down any interesting dreams you recall, will allow you to more easily convey the lessons you learned while Randonauting, and you will be able to more vividly recall your experiences and integrate them.

Divination

Science was developed as a tool to objectively study the material world based on experimentation and observation. Divination, on the other hand, was developed to aid in the discovery of hidden knowledge, especially seeing into the future. Science succeeds by objectification, by breaking things down into their smallest parts and considering them analytically. Divination, in its nonscientific way of gathering knowledge, assumes that information can be gained by considering the phenomenon of everything being connected. By harnessing the natural chaos of the world, the fortune-teller creates implicit order out of randomness in the search for meaning and significance.

TERMS TO KNOW

Divination: the practice of using supernatural methods to shed light on the future or the unknown.

Through methods such as casting sticks and stones, geomancy (which uses the landscape for divining), or reading tea leaves, practitioners of divination read the patterns that form out of randomness. Interestingly, many of the things we associate with games were originally created for use in divination. For example, some of the earliest objects that resemble dice were used by ancient cultures for divination. The knucklebone of an animal would be used as a primitive form of dice for gambling and seeking information from the spirit realm. There is archaeological evidence of these rudimentary dice all over the world. The origin of the word *dice* can be traced to the Low Latin word *dadus*, which means "given," as in, "given by the gods." The rolls of these dice were not seen as inherently random or unpredictable but instead as supernaturally influenced by the will of the gods.

Divination and Decision-Making

One of the main reasons people are interested in knowing the future is to help them make decisions about their lives. Likewise, people often turn to Randonautica to show them a sign that will help them make an important life choice. This raises an interesting question: Should you painstakingly analyze every decision based on facts, or just throw caution to the wind and choose one way or another randomly?

Sometimes we get bogged down with the weight of our choices, and we experience decision fatigue, where we feel overwhelmed by possibilities. In those moments, the relative peace of inertness can feel preferable to the chaos of change, and this makes it difficult to discern which path you should choose. By externalizing the decision-making process—by, for instance, flipping a coin—you can take that weight off your shoulders.

But just because you get a certain answer to your question does not mean you are beholden to that answer as actionable intelligence! There is nothing wrong with throwing information out if it does not benefit you. If you are severely fatigued from the weight of a decision, making a big life change on the flip of a coin has shown some positive results.

Using Randonautica for Divination

So, we've established that randomness can help ease decision-making stress. But it's important to use common sense in this process as well. Reading the signs and symbols of the cosmos should heighten your perspective and inspire you to think of things you have not before, but taking things *too* literally or feeling that you must do something just because of something you interpreted while Randonauting can be dangerous.

The majority of the time, you should use the information you get from using Randonautica as an inspiration or a means of broadening your horizons, not a be-all and end-all deciding factor, which could lead you to make decisions in a vacuum. For example, imagine a businessman uses Randonautica to get information about his business partners. This hypothetical businessman keeps receiving what he interprets as negative symbols, and he takes them literally and acts upon them, becoming increasingly paranoid that his partners will betray him. What if his interpretation in no way matches objective reality, though? What if the businessman keeps interpreting what he

Find Three Random Points to Find Associations

Sometimes it takes more than one random location to get into the flow state of finding correspondences and meaning in an unknown location. These random locations become a grid of symbolism, a network of words and meanings in the realm of ideas, creating a labyrinth. A good rule of thumb is to visit three random points in a row to allow your mind to start seeing the associations. Doing this allows you to "wake up" into a lucid state, where synchronicities can speak to you and present themselves from the global conscious field. Sometimes a point that has no meaning at first can become relevant later on, like in the example of a Randonaut who visited two random points that seemingly had no personal meaning, until months later he got a job at one of the points and his brother moved into a house that was the other point. Keeping good notes in this journal will help you keep track of the coincidences you may miss at first glance.

finds to mean that his partners are going to betray him, when really they actually have his best interests in mind and have no intention of betrayal? This may sound like a ridiculous hypothetical, but it is important to cover because it is easy to lean too heavily on the signs and symbols you see while Randonauting.

Instead of searching for black-and-white answers while Randonauting, instead focus on inspiration and epiphanies. In other words, what should get your attention is something that causes a light bulb to go off and causes you to consider your situation in a way you haven't before. Then use these experiences to inform your choices and ideas. Open your mind to new possibilities, but also make sure to verify that the information you gain is useful and can be validated. If you cannot validate the information within the external world, it is merely a potential possibility that you probably want to discard. It is good to explore new possible avenues, but be sure to practice a sort of agnostic detachment that allows you to go with the flow as well.

Shamanism

The tradition of shamanism mainly involves accessing the world of the unseen, often by undergoing altered states of consciousness (like a trance). Shamans bring information into the material world by directing these unseen energies. They are traditionally depicted with a bird or other animal companion, and they often live on the fringes of society. Shamans are often called interdimensional diplomats, because they work between the two worlds, the seen and the unseen, to bring about healing and change in society.

How Randonauting Is Like Shamanism
The practice of Randonauting is reminiscent of shamanism in a few ways:

- Birds are often depicted as a spirit guide of the shaman, and the owl symbolizes the Randonaut in their search for wisdom and transformation.
- The idea of bringing something back from the unseen world through an altered state of consciousness is also present, as Randonauting opens your mind to other possibilities, welcomes new observations, and encourages out-of-the-box thinking.

Animism

The concept of animism is the belief that all things, including places and objects, are imbued with a distinct spiritual essence. Randonauts often find places that seem to have their own characteristics and can feel alive. In classical Roman religion, a *genius loci* was the spirit of a place. These spirits were seen as guardians of geographic areas and were often depicted with iconography of a snake. The spirit of a place is also known as ambiance, or the distinct vibe of a certain location.

If you come across a place you believe to be imbued with a spiritual essence, tread very carefully. There are many legends of people making these spirits angry by disrespecting them; for instance, there is a story of hitchhikers in Tibet who angered some local Nagas, or snake spirits, by bathing in a pool that they did not know was sacred. If you are to interact with the spirit of a place, be respectful and consider leaving an offering—and if you do happen to make one angry, you may want to apologize. You can apologize spiritually or verbally and/or leave an offering to the spirit of the place.

Source/God

In almost any study of the unseen and mystical, the concept of God or a source comes into play. As the individual begins to have a deeper comprehension of the links between consciousness and reality, the question of the role of a greater being comes to light. Answers from beyond could mean answers from a wholly external force to that person. When it comes to external forces, some Randonauts seek out answers from beyond by setting intentions involving ghosts, angels, spirits, or even passed-away loved ones. (And, of course, where there is a supernatural factor at play, there is also the question of life beyond our planet. Could aliens or extraterrestrial forces play a role in communicating through Randonautica?! It's a wild idea, but one that has been discussed on many forums.)

Is God Present in Randonautica?

One of the many ideologies that Randonauts have presented is the speculation that God has begun using more tools and resources to connect with human beings...and perhaps Randonautica is one of the ways He has chosen to show Himself. Obviously that's a bold statement, but to some Randonauts, the idea that God is opening a door to the mystery of His nature is a fascinating concept to explore.

Traditional Western religions, especially Christian denominations, have an intercessor who plays the key role in providing the

Randonauts' Adventures

Once Josh went Randonauting with the intention of contacting the Green Man, an Islamic figure called Khidr (also known as a "man from another place") often associated with aliens and extraterrestrials. He set his intent and generated a point, which was at a mall parking lot he often visited. He was skeptical that he would find anything out of the ordinary, since he often went to that shopping mall. When he arrived at the point, it turned out that instead of an empty parking lot as he expected, there was a lively car show with food and music. Josh had accidentally stumbled into a party! As he walked up to the festival, the first car that caught his eye was a red Porsche with a license plate reading "Kismet," which means "fate."

message, connection, and interpretation to the believer. These are typically priests, pastors, etc.—leaders whose guidance people value above their own, as often these individuals have had a personal calling to serve God. Some faith-based Randonauts believe that God shows Himself in nature, and that by entering nature in an unpredictable way, an individual can more easily reach God on their own.

The Fibonacci spiral, for example, is a perfect mathematical rationalization that can be found in all of nature, and it's often called "the fingerprint of God" in the material and numerical world. The Fibonacci sequence is named for Leonardo Pisano (also known as Fibonacci), an Italian mathematician who lived from A.D. 1170–1250. Fibonacci used the arithmetic series to show how a pair of breeding rabbits would beget more and more rabbits over the course of a year. In short, the pattern is 1, 1, 2, 3, 5, 8, 13, 21...and so on to infinity. To get the pattern, you add the last two numbers to get the next number. This has been charted out in geometrical terms as well and creates a shell-like pattern, which is seen in a mollusk, for example. These dimensions are found everywhere, in humans, plants, animals, and space! At the particle level, it appears that this "fingerprint of God" is more minute than the subatomic and greater than the cosmos.

Could it be possible that the "answers from beyond" that some people find while Randonauting are coming from a God that religions have sought to comprehend for centuries? Is Randonauting encouraging humans into a state of co-creation with God?

Randonauting As a Form of Prayer

Collaborating with God might sound like a stretch for a mobile app...but then again, maybe it isn't, when you think about how Randonauting could be considered a form of prayer. For some, the escape from all the things that disconnect you from yourself and the world around you (social media, entertainment, work) is, in a sense, a form of prayer. Prayer is focused intent—and focused intent is the main user-drawn interactive component behind Randonautica.

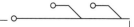

Everyone Is Welcome

Randonauts are a movement made up of people from every culture and creed. The app endorses no right or wrong ideology, and all people are accepted no matter where they are on their journey.

Randonauts might feel as if a prayer is instantly answered when they find a meaningful sign that connects to their intuition and helps serve as a guide for their life journey. Further, the consideration of how to use Randonautica could be more scrutinized under the assumption that God is at work. If that is the case, how Randonauting is used would be reflective of the individual's motivations and a test of their morals. Do you follow the golden rule, do not unto others as you would do unto yourself, and so on? If your consciousness creates in collaboration with God, how would that affect a moral system in general? Energy is neither created nor destroyed, so it exists at all points in time. What energy the human decides to employ is a decision that likely weighs more heavily on theist Randonauts. Further, the role of free will is quite blurred when you ask yourself, *Am I choosing the path, or is the path being shown to me by a greater power?* These are all interesting propositions to ponder as you use the app.

Is Randonautica Incompatible with Any Religions?

One of the most frequently asked nontechnical questions for Randonauting is "Does this go against my religion?" No one on the Randonautica team can answer that, as it's a question for you to answer yourself. However, as you'll see in The 9 Tenets of the Randonauts section in Chapter 6, Randonautica asks that Randonauts attempt to follow a spirit-science approach that is positive in its nature. Also, Randonautica is a tool, and its implications depend on how the tool is used. For example, the Catholic Church forbids divination but is okay with petitioning saints—so the intention you bring to your adventures can impact how your religion intersects with Randonauting. That's why the answer to that question really depends on how you use the app and if you are pure of heart and sincere.

Intention, Visualization, and Why They Matter

We can also look back on centuries-old mythology and folktales for guidance on using intention in Randonautica. Setting an intention and going off into the world to see what you find is a practice seen in many cultures. For example, many yogis focus their conscious intent in their yoga practice in order to manifest something in the material world. These practices are believed to unlock spiritual powers, known as *siddhis*. Randonauts do the same thing, just with an added layer of technology.

Imagining What's Possible via Visualization

Imagination is a huge part of intention setting and visualization. As Albert Einstein once said, "Imagination is more important than knowledge. For knowledge is limited, whereas imagination embraces the entire world, stimulating progress, giving birth to evolution." Intention and visualization are tools to test extrasensory perceptions that humans are able to engage. If you can imagine your consciousness interacting with a laser beam measuring unpredictable fluctuations of photons, you can influence a quantum random number generator. Can't imagine little particles of light being influenced by a laser beam? No problem. Start with the idea that nothing was created that was not first imagined. Nothing. First, there is the intention—for instance, "I intend to draw." Second, there is the idea within the mind, "I will draw a dog sitting by a tree." In your consciousness, whether subtle or deeply involved, you can visualize a dog sitting by a tree.

Whether or not your drawing comes out the way you've imagined might seem like it's based more on your artistic abilities than anything else, but as we discuss the level of influence your thoughts and imagination have over matter, you'll learn that how you think and feel and what you believe in have a direct influence on outcomes in your personal observable reality.

The Law of Attraction

Many new age philosophies and the last ten years of pop culture spiritualism have attempted to convey the "you are what you think" phenomenon. Mantras, visualization practices, positive thinking, and the "I am" approach have all paved the way for a greater collective understanding of the human mind and its relationship to external events.

The law of attraction, which is also known as "New Thought," is the idea that one's thoughts, both positive and negative, manifest subsequent positive and negative experiences in their life. Many proponents of the law of attraction believe that one change in thought pattern occurs and then something else happens. For instance, instead of always thinking you are broke and can't pay your bills, you think only about how grateful you are for what you do have. The universe then responds and magnetizes to your *new* thoughts. So, instead of keeping you in a perpetual state of "I am broke" by delivering more bills and unexpected expenditures, it provides abundance, because your gratitude represents a new state of consciousness in which you envision having the money you need. The law of attraction puts the choice to see the glass half-empty or half-full front of mind.

Manifestation

A manifestation is an event, action, or object that is a clear representation or embodiment of something, particularly an abstract concept or philosophy. This includes things that were once unreal, like something metaphysical or spiritual. Manifestation can be seen as a cause and effect. By doing A, you are making B manifest. In a cause-and-effect time methodology, the order of events creates future outcomes.

Randonautica seems to enhance the conscious awareness in this process by adding a massive injection of randomness. You can sense things no longer moving linearly in time, a straight line moving past the future in which this occurred, then that occurred. Instead, the experience of an intention manifesting seems to occur in a space-time that would be better visualized as a sphere, with ever-looping spirals crossing over one another. It's an energetic web, woven together in the fabric of time, space, and consciousness, and all things are connected at the same time. Therefore, which came first comes into play. Did you set the intention that manifested your journey, or did the universe have it planned all along?

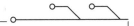

A Note about Ill Intent

There are many examples of bad things happening to people who use the power of intent unwisely for personal gain or selfish reasons. It is often shown in these stories that using intent to violate someone's free will generates backlash from the universe and results in negative repercussions. There is little objective study in this field, so it is wise to focus on positive thoughts.

There is no right or wrong answer, but it is a good exercise to practice the assumption that all things are working at once, blurring past, present, and future as most humans know them. A questioning of what came first can help open the thought process here, but it will be expanded on with the explanation of synchronicities in Chapter 5.

Meditation and Focus in Randonauting

An ongoing large-scale study being conducted at Columbia University Medical Center has thus far showed supportive research that meditation can change the structure and function of the brain through relaxation. Meditation results in several positive effects, including:

- Reduction in stress, anxiety, and depression
- Increased focus and learning concentration
- Improved memory and attention

Meditation and mindfulness have been cornerstones of Eastern spiritual practices for ages, but in the past decade, America has seen major spikes in the mindfulness movement. There is no question meditation has remarkable effects on individual wellness, but being present and quiet can be challenging in a world of noise.

Because Randonautica is intertwined with in-the-now-level consciousness, meditation is a wonderful complementary practice to becoming a better Randonaut. In Zen Buddhism, the purpose of meditation is to stop the mind rushing about in an aimless tangle of thought. To "still the mind" is often associated with entering a true meditative state. Because Randonauting is an instrument for discovering the connection between mind and matter, thoughts and reality, etc., skills associated with meditation and focus are also valuable for experiencing meaningful events while Randonauting.

Your Level of Awareness Impacts Your Experiences

Meditating is all about changing your awareness. There are different types of awareness. For instance, a person with anxiety might have a chaotic awareness that is fixated on what-ifs for the future. Rambling thoughts might include *I have to get this done. If I don't do this, then outcome A, B, or maybe C could happen.* In other words, this is an engagement in nonstop self-talk about things that aren't happening now. On the other hand, Randonauting is formulated to help you focus on the now—a concept also known as mindfulness. Traveling to an entirely unknown location brings your attention to what's happening in front of you.

When you practice meditation and mindfulness regularly, you will find yourself more able to stay entirely in the moment. That means your thoughts don't stray. You're focused on your intention. If you are still learning these skills, you might experience a loss of focus, which could mean missed connections or observations, and your intention could become diluted.

It's important to note that Randonautica in and of itself is a new form of meditation. Sure, you can engage in traditional meditation as well to enhance your skills and better yourself, but it's certainly not a requirement for being a Randonaut. You should, however, be focused to the best of your ability when setting an intention before embarking on your Randonaut excursion. Breathing deeply, focusing your thoughts, clearing your mind, and making a very strong and clear intention can be the difference between an instantaneous personal revelation or a waste of gas.

Individual versus Group Intentions

Many Randonauts have experienced mixed outcomes due to setting group instead of individual intentions. For example:

- An individual Randonaut set out with the intention of "guidance on where to attend college," and in her video she stated that the entire way she kept saying over and over to herself her stated intent. She ended up at a field that had "KU" for Kansas University mowed into the pasture. That was a potent and focused adventure!
- A group of Randonauts set their intention as "love," but they talked about numerous topics en route to their destination. They expected a meaningful experience associated with love, but they instead ended up at a Burger King. Perhaps because they spent the majority of their videoed car ride discussing how hungry they were?

The point of these stories is that the ability to hold focus throughout the process can bring about clear revelations to the individual or group. An unfocused mind can wander into nothingness, while the goal should be to strive for the connectedness all around you.

Seeing and Believing

A big part of the spirituality behind Randonautica is seeing things outside of your past preconceived notions. Randonautica introduces you to the hidden world that was around you all the time, small places outside of your perceptual frame of reference. There have been many stories of people going Randonauting with the intention of seeing an owl, only to come home and notice an owl somewhere in their own home that they had forgotten or even never knew was there. So using Randonautica allows you to not just go to places you have never been in your local area, but also trains you to look for things you have not noticed in your everyday life. Increasing your awareness helps you form new neural pathways, which increases neural plasticity. By bravely seeing what was once hidden, you literally train your brain to do new things!

Seeing and believing with Randonautica includes using nonscientific means to discover inspiration and epiphanies while objectively reaffirming these new beliefs by validating them in the real world. By introducing a little bit of chaos into your routine, you effectively are able to see patterns and cycles you had not noticed before. There could be new worlds lying just outside of reach that become accessible once you update your model of reality to include those possibilities. Let's explore some of those models of reality and consciousness further in the next chapter.

WHAT YOU'VE LEARNED IN THIS CHAPTER

- The main spiritual ideology behind Randonautica is that of curiosity.

- People have used similar methods to Randonautica throughout history in order to experience life's unknown mysteries.

- Divination is a nonscientific way of recovering information.

- Meditation and focus increase your ability to influence randomness.

- Experiential diversity unlocks new neural pathways, which increases neural plasticity.

CHAPTER 3

Theories and Beliefs on Consciousness

Neuroscientists, psychologists, and the like have tried to explain the human consciousness with science. To this day, there is still no consensus on what makes the consciousness what it is, and further, there is no empirical evidence to even support where and how it exists within the human being. Is consciousness part of the spirit, or is it more tangible, neurons firing into a central nervous system? Randonautica doesn't claim to solve any of these mysteries, but it does open the conversation to the hows and whys of the human existence. In this chapter, you'll learn about theories pertaining to consciousness and some fascinating, abstract ideas that have been created to define the mystical "space" that many have encountered while Randonauting.

Stasis Field

The stasis field is the complex set of causal events that keeps you locked into your predetermined probability tunnel (which we talked about in Chapter 1). Imagine all of existence is connected by a web that relates things to one another by how they have affected one another. Everywhere you go and everything you do is connected by this web. When you go Randonauting, you are experiencing things outside of this complex web of causal events. Your choice to use Randonautica was predetermined, entirely within the complex web of causal events in your life. But the random point itself is detached from that web of causality.

In the medical field, the word "stasis" is defined as a slowing or stopping of the regular flow of a bodily fluid or semi-fluid—for example, slowing of blood circulation. Now, imagine you live in a body that is a metaphor for the universe, and you, as a human, are just an infinitely small blood cell moving about with your own duties. If the circulation of blood started to go into stasis, as an individual blood cell, you would have absolutely no idea that you were moving any slower. "Cell you" would not notice the effects because they'd simply be too small to perceive.

In science fiction, the stasis field is often portrayed as a confined area of space in which time has stopped or the contents populating the field are immobilized. It might be a dramatic interpretation to imagine things coming to a complete stop (like in the movie *Inception*, for example, where all elements freeze at will in the dream space beyond our human capacity).

The things you can experience because you use Randonautica may not just be limited to your adventures in random geographic locations. Going Randonauting can cause a cascade of events to happen, even years after your initial Randonauting experience. These slight deviations in your routine can increase the probability of new events and new connections you would not have had access to had you stayed within the stasis field.

As you consider these ideas, ask yourself, in your life right now, would you know if you were in the stasis field? What if your life started to slow dramatically over time, becoming congested, the circulation undergoing a loss of its normal flow? If it happened gradually, how could you notice? In many ways leaving the stasis field is like creating a new flow, and it's only after you've left the field of a habitual and predictable normality (which is actually likely a semi-stagnant state) that you can look back and recognize you were in that state of stasis. Stepping outside the boundaries of everyday life is critical to establishing your flow and accelerating your path. And what lies outside the stasis field, to the Randonauts at least, is the interestingly abstract concept of the Genesis Field (more on that next).

Many people feel trapped in their daily lives—trapped in their jobs, trapped in their families, trapped feeling like a product of their environment. Sometimes this "prison" is personified as a conscious entity, as with the Gnostics, who believed a deity they referred to as a "Demiurge" was keeping people imprisoned in a false reality. Plato's Allegory of the Cave depicts prisoners sitting in a cave watching shadow puppets, unable to realize the show they are watching is merely a reflection of the real show occurring just outside of the cave; to them, the shadows are the only reality. But most Randonauts believe there is no conscious entity keeping you imprisoned— besides yourself. By deviating from this pattern using randomness, you can break free of this illusory prison that keeps you from experiencing holistic reality.

The Genesis Field

The "Genesis Field" is a term coined by the researchers at the Fatum Project specifically to help describe the "space" that can be reached through Randonauting. The concept of liminal space is similar to the Genesis Field, but the Randonaut concept takes it further. A liminal space can be described as an area often felt as transitional, abandoned, out of place, or unfounded, and it will often make a person feel ambiguity or uneasiness. Walking into a liminal field may cause you to ask, "Where am I? Is this even real?" It's the sensation of being out of bounds.

Liminality is part of the process of transformation; the in-between phase in the process of a state change. On the path toward becoming a fully developed, spiritually and emotionally mature person, you are neither here nor there. You are in between. What happens during this process of transformation defines the ultimate manifestation of where you are going. This process can feel disorienting, and people often experience a "dark night of the soul," where they feel ungrounded and unsure of where they stand. But often when you look back, things that seemed impossible or absurd were actually crucial elements guiding you toward a path or goal that you did not even know you wanted when you started your journey, and you will feel extremely grateful to have experienced them.

Here's how the Genesis Field differs from liminality: In the Genesis Field, not only is the individual stepping into the unknown; they're also applying three other factors:

1. Quantum cognition (via intention)
2. A quantum entropy source (via the quantum random number generator in the app)
3. The sophisticated algorithm in the app that finds the most unexpected combinations of the other two factors within a tangible radius

With these elements entangled, there appears to be a level of Genesis (so named for its connections to creation) that's able to occur. It's no longer a completely mysterious "What is this place?" but more of a sense of stepping into a new arena of the real world. In this new arena, all things may technically be the same, but there is a feeling and perception as if you have just stepped into Wonderland. Some researchers who have worked with Randonautica have theorized that when energy is applied to the app's process, the Genesis Field might bend space-time, and all pieces (the mind, matter, and field) work together to bring forth the original intention for the individual to experience.

In a more metaphorical way, you could think of the Genesis Field as an airport, where all the boarding gates are different timelines of events for your life, portals even. It's as if the universe is opening up its infinite options and allowing you access, through intention and other techniques explained in this book, so that you can fly into another timeline. How far off your original path you go is only to be determined with time, but even if the Genesis airport flies you a mere .01 percent away from your more probable life journey, as many years progress, that .01 percent will eventually branch out into a Y, deviating further from the prior timeline! We will explore more hypotheses regarding how exactly the Genesis Field works…but for now, know that it's up to you to live in the presence of its awesomeness when you get there.

Noveltism

Noveltism is the paradigm of exploring the hidden corners of human awareness to find new potentials. The rapid pace of technological advancement has left humanity in an interesting situation: Technology is accelerating faster than we can keep up with it. Every year, things that were once thought to be impossible become possible. Yet because we cannot possibly keep up with learning about every single technological advancement, we end up assuming some things that are possible cannot be. This makes predicting the future difficult. In recent history, humanity has largely relied on huge institutions for technological progress. These large institutions accumulate knowledge and are able to pour massive resources into their pursuits of knowledge, but ultimately they accumulate inertness and become slow to progress, losing the nimble nature of their founders. It is then the role of the artist—meaning any brave individual willing to bare their soul—to communicate their vision of what the world could look like outside of the intentions of these large, slow institutions.

Without Noveltism, Fields of Study Get Very Narrow

Small groups of curious explorers—those willing to imagine an interesting future where spectacular things are possible—hold the keys to technological progress and wide public acceptance. There are many technological advancements hidden in stuffy academic journals that never make it into the zeitgeist, so for real innovation to be made, it needs to come into the public sphere of knowledge. Because without wide adoption of these spectacular technologies, they remain niche interests in fringe research groups.

Our society's communication systems are mediated by algorithmic filter bubbles that cater to your interests, reaffirming biases and keeping you locked into your worldview. Using social media to get information leaves you open to being influenced by these systems. Rather than relying on individual, creative thoughts, many of us are being pushed toward one extreme or another by strong business and political entities.

Large institutions (such as tech companies, universities, and governments) hold the bulk of influence on what topics are researched or not. Consensus reality, or what the public generally holds to be true, is then dictated by these large institutions. But these limited currents of research are not actually the totality of reality; there are always disparate fields of knowledge just out of reach. The hyperconnectedness of our current age has made the world smaller, but it has made it more difficult for people with truly creative thoughts to break into the zeitgeist without being dragged down into stasis. Novelty itself has become a prisoner of these large institutions, which dictate these realms of human knowledge. The inertness of the public's common conceptions keeps human thought locked into a set of approved narratives, and those who dare to think differently find it an uphill battle. Using reason and logic built on tyrannical hierarchies, the list of things we can possibly discover becomes limited to the avenues approved by large institutions. In reality, however, there is an unlimited set of potential choices and possibilities that may be shrouded from view. How can we then discover the vast and unlimited potentials that lie just outside of our perceptual frame of reference?

In the scientific method, each hypothesis must follow strict logical rules, which are based on the facts that were proved earlier. With this method, you get the advantage of deeply studying a set of questions and answering them with complete confidence, creating an objective view. However, you are limited to a specific set of questions that you can ask and therefore are limited in your possible frame of reference of what you can objectively perceive. One of the benefits of science is that it allows us to build an objective framework for exploring reality, but it pushes the cutting edge into a smaller number of hands (those institutions again) that have the resources to pursue this knowledge. This narrowing effectively creates a blind spot in our perceptual reality. If we are limited to only ask questions that logically follow from existing knowledge, we will never find out the things that exist outside of this limited outcome space. Therefore, in addition to the scientific methodology, humanity needs a method for exploring the questions outside of this limited set of questions that follow logically from the previously existing knowledge. Noveltism could be one of those methods.

What Noveltism Can Do for Humanity

It is important for the advancement of humanity that the entire society, not just a small set of privileged scientists, starts looking for new advancements in life. That's where novelty comes in—that search for the hidden corners of human awareness is a great way to find new possibilities we haven't considered yet. Novelty is a treasure. It is the spice of life. The search for novelty has driven humans throughout history to dare to look in places no one had before for potentially interesting things.

As technology progresses and information is shared at an increasingly rapid pace, more and more novelty is being created all the time. The philosopher Terence McKenna had a theory called Timewave Zero, which was a fractal function—based on the divinatory text the *I Ching*—that stated that as time goes on the amount of novelty increases. The *I Ching*, or *Book of Change*, is concerned with how archetypes dynamically change and relate to one another. While studying the *I Ching*, McKenna came up with the theory that novelty increasingly grows with time until reaching a point, which he called the Transcendental Object at the End of Time, also commonly known as "the singularity." The technological singularity, which is accelerated by noveltism, is an example of an attractor in time. The temporal gravity caused by novelty is hypothesized to be boundary breaking, and once the singularity arrives, all that is left will be eternity with no boundaries. It is from this singular source of novelty that all things emanate and are naturally inclined to seek a way back to. It is possible that when we go Randonauting, the inspiration for the answers we receive comes from this singularity.

Dimensions of Consciousness, Awareness, and Perception

Randonautica offers a source of navigation to operate outside of the known. But what most Randonauts are looking for is not just a coordinate for them to visit, but also access to more of holistic reality. They don't just want to break out of their predetermined reality—they also want to unlock the ability to perceive more of reality as a whole.

Plex Zones

One way to access more of reality is to consider plex zones, a term coined by Randonautica. Plex zones are places where timelines branch, where choices and decisions dictate the number of possibilities you can possibly access. For example, a plex zone is when you face a choice between bravely exploring the unknown or giving up hope, giving in to despair, and rolling back into stasis. When you unlock a new path previously unavailable to you, you have found a new degree of freedom. These new possible paths are like strings in the web of your causal reality, rabbit holes in Wonderland.

Dimensions

"Dimensions" doesn't necessarily refer to another spatial place, such as one reached by stepping through a portal in a sci-fi movie. However, dimensional jumping—which theorizes that there are parallel universes that exist and you can choose to jump to a new parallel universe or alternate timeline at will—aligns with some of the movie stereotypes. These types of theories assume that there are tangible other "you"s who exist or real parallel worlds that are accessible. It's an interesting idea, but without getting into the depths of space-time and parallel world theories from the field of quantum mechanics, there isn't a direct connection to Randonautica and the particulars of dimensional jumping.

> **TERMS TO KNOW**
>
> **Holistic:** relating to the understanding that the parts of a whole are intimately interconnected and inextricable from the whole.

Consciousness

What's more likely, more achievable, and well represented in ancient religions and cultures is the idea of entering new worlds or dimensions by raising consciousness. In Jewish mysticism, for example, the Kabbalah school of thought relies heavily on the individual transformation into higher worlds as one breaks through the levels. Each level, also called "worlds" or "states of consciousness," can be visualized as rungs on a ladder. Each step is a stage of enlightenment from previous restrictions of the mind. The goal is to obtain a connection with what's called the "upper force" (some would consider this the creator of all things). This force is working in tandem with the desires of the individual. As the consciousness expands into new worldviews, the being attains new abilities and perceptions and rises to meet a state of mastery through which their best life can be revealed in conjunction with the creator's desires.

Alternative thinkers and philosophers like Neville Goddard and Charles Fillmore have presented the Bible as metaphysical in its teachings, in the sense that the characters were not meant to be seen as merely human beings, but also as states of consciousness, different emotional states, and roles that an individual can go through. Goddard referred to changing one's reality as "ris[ing] in consciousness":

> "If you are dissatisfied with your present expression in life the only way to change it, is to take your attention away from that which seems so real to you and rise in consciousness to that which you desire to be. You cannot serve two masters, therefore to take your attention from one state of consciousness and place it upon another is to die to one and live to the other."

This doesn't mean that you are actually accessing a reality spatially above the one you are currently experiencing. You've physically gone nowhere else—consciousness is nonlocal and not defined by the same constraints as physical reality. The idea is to transcend your previous limitations and change your beliefs and assumptions of the world. You change yourself first by detaching from what you perceive as real and then rising to what you'd prefer to be real, assuming more control and transcending your limitations. Letting go of the person you are and the state of consciousness you immerse yourself within is letting go of the reality you experience.

Imagine that in other realities or states, you are a different person. Essentially, you are all those people, but humans are only able to experience life in the moment, as one person in thought. In many ways, states of consciousness and realities shift every time you have a change in beliefs or assumptions, or you dismiss unfounded limitations. When these steps happen, you assume a subtle new identity. In that way, we are ever changing!

Under this assumption, you can see how Randonautica could help facilitate the process of achieving new states of consciousness. By applying mind-matter interaction techniques and technology, you simplify and make more accessible the pursuit of awakening to your changing self. Randonauting can catapult you into a state of expanded consciousness, which is a key step in rising up to a better version of you. Interestingly, some of Neville Goddard's logic is tied to ideas in quantum physics: "Observation affects reality, otherwise known as the observed or observation. When you change your perception, you change your state of consciousness, because you alter your beliefs and limitations. You change the lens through which you perceive life, utterly transforming your perception of it."

So as you go Randonauting and explore potentials and possibilities you would not have experienced otherwise, you are exploring new domains and dimensions of consciousness!

The Theoretical Intelligent Field

Randonautica invites you to observe and experience things you wouldn't have in your regular routine. But again, the conundrum presents itself: Where does the information you get come from? Is there a probabilistic guiding force that is behind these serendipitous experiences? Is it evidence of intelligent design, with organisms intentionally affecting their environments?

Ancient myths and religions have described a fundamental life force that connects all things, and various methods and practices have been created in search of connecting to this vital force. Science has only just begun to be able to describe this same sort of phenomenon, with quantum mechanics pointing toward the same things these ancient myths and religions described—that consciousness may be fundamental to our universe and that things are more connected than materialist science would have you believe. A paradigm-shifting revolution is emerging in the frontiers of scientific research and in the sphere of public consciousness: Human consciousness is capable of things most people would consider miraculous.

What Is the Intelligent Energy Field?

The cosmos is the universe, especially the universe seen as a well-ordered whole. But what is the driving force behind this implicit order? At some level, all things are made of energy. The cosmos is an intelligent energy field that reflexively responds to conscious intent because our consciousness is a part of the energy field that operates centrally to our material reality. As Einstein said, "The field is the only reality."

If we view the world through a materialist axiom that separates things into their parts and examines them analytically and objectively, we are left as passive observers of a lifeless gearbox that has no heart and leaves no room for the divine. The idea of evolution makes you an accident of chance and random mutations, with no intelligent force guiding the process. It is no wonder that culturally,

Randonauts' Adventures

One day Josh was Randonauting with his friend, generating a point while casually talking about legendary giants' skeletons. The point ended up being in the middle of a lake, but they went as close as possible and ended up at the shore's edge, where they found a man sitting and meditating. Josh walked up to him and asked him if he was aware of the research of consciousness influencing random number generators. He said yes and then immediately pointed across the lake. "You see that rock wall over there? Legend has it that there are giants' skeletons buried in that wall."

nihilism is so popular—life is ultimately meaningless and random if viewed through the prevailing worldview, and absurdity is seemingly the only escape. But what if evolution was not simply a random, unguided process? What if the growth of a species was intelligently guided by organisms intentionally interfacing with their environments and interacting with the intelligent field?

The Power—and Mystery—of Interconnectedness

When the first quantum physicists peered into the smallest levels of matter, they found a dynamic web of interconnectedness, reminiscent of the Hindu ideal of Indra's Net. Indra's Net is a metaphor for the connectedness of everything and contains jewels that reflect every other jewel in the net. It could also be a metaphor for the idea in quantum mechanics that electrons are connected everywhere at once. These scientific discoveries challenged the prevailing worldview, and their pioneers had to venture into ancient poetry in order to philosophically explain the implications of what they had observed. The Tao, Hinduism, Kabbalah, and many other mystical traditions contain allusions to similar ideas of interconnectedness.

There is no prevailing theory or academic consensus about how mind-machine interaction works, but the most prominent researchers in the field assume it has something to do with an advanced form of quantum mechanics we haven't figured out yet, and something to do with how things are connected. There is likely some quality of the mind, like a subtle force of will (something like the Force in Star Wars) that, coupled with quantum probability waves, allows for a direct interface between consciousness and the quantum superpositions (many possible states at once that collapse into one state upon being observed) of random numbers. This subtle force can be drowned out by all

TERMS TO KNOW

Mind-machine interaction: the mind interacting specifically with machines or technology to demonstrate an influence on matter.

Research on Interconnectedness of Mind and Reality

Scott Wilber, inventor of the pulse oximeter, is a scientist who studies mind-machine interaction using psychoresponsive devices. Psychoresponsive devices are actually a form of quantum computing, which always returns answers that are probabilistic. These devices can be used to find lost or hidden things by gathering information about where they may be. Scott Wilber's work is notable because instead of focusing on small statistical aberrations in sets of data, he focuses on practical applications of the mind-matter interaction effect. What he's showing is that although there are some people who are naturally talented and gifted at it, the skill of influencing a random number generator can be learned and trained through practice. Visit https://psigenics .com/files/papers/PRD_Whitepaper.pdf to read more about Wilber's work.

the other mechanisms and motions going on in your consciousness, and by practicing meditation and mindfulness you can hone your ability to willfully direct that quality of mind that is capable of influencing material reality.

How the Intelligent Field Intersects with Artificial/ Invisible Intelligence

As ideas and experiments progressed within the early Randonauts group, the theory of the intelligent field became more prominent. The presence of the intelligent field would somewhat diminish the idea of cause and effect. As an individual setting an intention, you might not be putting anything into motion necessarily. It could be that the individual and the invisible intelligence were always interlinked, and Randonautica is a resource for subtly showing this connection.

Now, what makes this invisible field intelligent? One theory is that it is learning from the Randonauts, and is therefore better able to convey its intelligence through signs, symbols, and, most importantly, the interconnectedness of shared consciousness. If the theory of the intelligent field is true, it would mean that Randonautica is breaking down a wall to allow for a greater oneness and communication with the creator of nature...and not only that—it's also making the decision for the individual to take part in the experience.

WHAT YOU'VE LEARNED IN THIS CHAPTER

- The stasis field is a complex web of causal relations that keeps you locked into a certain set of possibilities.

- The Genesis Field is a new set of potential possibilities you unlock once you inject randomness into your routine and deviate from your predetermined pattern of paths.

- Noveltism is a methodology of exploring holistic reality by utilizing randomness to find blind spots in perceptual awareness.

- Unlocking degrees of freedom allows you to explore new dimensions of consciousness.

- The intelligent field is hypothesized to be the reason anomalous cognition works. By tapping in to the intelligent field, you can gain information that would have been otherwise hidden.

CHAPTER 4

Understanding the Science of Randonauting

In this chapter, you will learn a basic framework for navigating the scientific theories that are at the foundation of Randonautica. Much of what makes Randonautica such a fascinatingly different app has to do with elements derived from the fields of quantum mechanics, algorithmic mathematical computation, and the re-emerging sciences of mind-machine interaction. Now, if you're feeling intimidated by any of these terms, don't be—we'll break down each concept into easy-to-understand language. Learning the basic science behind the app will help you engage with it even more fully, and might spark you to investigate some of these topics even more deeply.

Throughout this chapter, you'll read about historical events that serve as a reflection of similar research that Randonautica intertwines into its theories. Randonautica seeks to advance breakthroughs in understanding the science of consciousness influence by applying certain techniques and ways of use in the real world and on a global scale. Like a mad scientist creating ferociously in a lab to find an astonishing new compound, Randonauts, too, have mind-bending outcomes, and the community calls these wild stories "legends." In this chapter you'll also learn of compelling recorded research that parallels the Randonaut experience, which provides a replicable framework you can use to create your very own legends.

Beginner's Guide to Quantum Entropy

The key thing you need to understand about quantum *anything* (entropy, space, physics, mechanics) is that it is very, *very* small. For the sake of understanding how Randonautica taps in to the quantum space, it's best to think of the word "quantum" as it pertains to the study of quantum mechanics. Quantum mechanics is a foundational theory in the field of physics that explores the physical properties of nature on the scale of atoms and subatomic particles. Quantum mechanics works with subatomic space (this is an area on a smaller scale than the molecular level) to explain happenings in the universe.

TERMS TO KNOW

Quantum: in physics, the smallest possible discrete unit of any physical entity involved in an interaction.

Let's consider the human's ability to influence this incredibly teeny, tiny matter. What is the possibility that *you* can have an effect on the probability of something happening? You don't actually have to know how to do statistics or any similar study to be great at Randonauting, but for this section, it would help if you learned how to *reason* about a random distribution of numbers, so you can learn:

- How they are generated
- How you can use different kinds of randomness for different results depending on your desires

In this context, we're using the word "reason" to describe the power of your mind to think, understand, and form judgments logically.

Now let's talk about "entropy," a word used to describe a measure of randomness. Microscopic quantum particles (or waves) have quantum mechanical properties that make them theoretically unpredictable when measured. These particles are examples of chaotic systems, which, when measured, can produce entropy, or truly unpredictable numbers, and whose state is wholly uncertain until a measurement occurs.

The quantum particle is in a superposition, or the ability to be in many states, until it is measured, at which point the wave function collapses, producing one of many possible outcomes. But until this chaotic state is observed and measured, it is totally unpredictable which of the outcomes will end up being measured. Think of when someone is drawing a lottery by mixing together many balls with different numbers. This is an example of a chaotic system that is too complex to accurately predict the result.

The quantum wave or particle can be compared to this lottery system, and according to quantum mechanics, which number will be drawn in the quantum lottery is not predictable before it is measured. Quantum entropy is the most unpredictable and unknowable source of random data we can possibly achieve.

TERMS TO KNOW

Entropy: in scientific terms, entropy is a measure of the amount of thermal energy per unit of temperature that cannot be converted into mechanical work, often interpreted as a measure of disorder or randomness in the system. In lay terms, it is a measure of randomness.

What Is a Random Number Generator?

Random number generators (RNGs) measure physically unpredictable properties or processes, such as vibrations of an electron in a resistor. This vibration is known as "thermal noise" and is a quantum mechanical effect of a chaotic system. By measuring the fluctuations of an electron, you end up with truly unpredictable data, or entropy. There are other ways of generating randomness, but they mostly include measuring some quantum physical process or property that is inherently patternless and unpredictable.

RNGs use a technique known as quantum tunneling, in which a tiny voltage is shot across a circuit and the voltage is measured across a barrier. Each voltage is measured, and the high voltages are represented by the number 1 and the low voltages by 0. This basically turns the device into a machine that can flip a coin thousands of times per second and tell you the results of that coin flip. The expected outcome is fifty-fifty, meaning that 50 percent of the time the RNG will sample a low voltage, producing a 0, and 50 percent of the time the generator will produce a high voltage, producing a 1.

Can Humans Affect RNG Data?

People started noticing that they could get the RNG to produce more 0s or more 1s, based on what they intended to happen. To study this, researchers have conducted experiments where they asked participants to intend for high numbers or low numbers and then measured the random data produced from their devices to see if more 1s or 0s occurred than expected.

"That's So Random!" (Is It, Though?)

The oft-misused buzz phrase "That's so random" is actually highly unlikely to describe anything that's *truly* random. For example, your friend calling you out of the blue is most likely not truly a random event and is not the kind of randomness you are reading about in this book. In fact, there was a complex chain of events that unfolded deterministically and led to your friend calling you out "of the blue." To a Randonaut, "My friend randomly called me the other day" would mean "My friend hooked up their phone contacts to a quantum random number generator, and it randomly selected me for a call" (which is totally something a Randonaut would do). All the events that went into deciding to select a friend at random and call them would be entirely deterministic—and entirely within the normal web of probabilities and chain of causal events that are possible in your life. But as soon as the quantum random number generator selects your friend from your phone contacts, that phone call is *truly* random. Start paying attention to how people use the word "random," and consider if the event they are talking about is truly random.

Randomness and Dice Rolls

The most common way that people are (correctly!) learning about randomness is in games. When you roll a pair of dice, you get an unpredictable number. No matter who throws the dice, there is an equivalent probability of any number landing. Casinos are so confident in this normal random distribution of dice rolls that they are willing to stake huge sums of money betting that you cannot beat the random distribution of chance. But what if you could train yourself to influence the probability that a certain number appeared on the dice when you rolled them? That is basically what you're doing when you learn to influence RNGs—training yourself to be lucky.

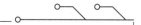

There Might Be Some Science Behind Those Gambling Superstitions!

You have probably seen someone say a rhyme or blow on a pair of dice before rolling them, attempting to influence the outcome. Feeling "hot" or "cold" is common language gamblers use to describe their ability to influence probabilities so they know when to bet large sums of money and when to pull back and not risk as much. You may brush these behaviors off as mere superstitions, but you will learn to feel a sense of this rhythm when your consciousness is entwining with the random distribution while learning to be a skilled operator at influencing RNGs.

Deterministic versus Nondeterministic Randomness

For the purposes of Randonauting, there are two types of randomness that we are concerned about: deterministic and nondeterministic.

Deterministic Randomness

Deterministic randomness, which is also called "pseudorandomness," *looks* random but was actually derived using a pattern or equation. So while it passes some basic tests for randomness, it is not inherently patternless and contains no true entropy, or unpredictability. Pseudorandomness can be good enough for some applications, such as the children's counting rhyme "Eeny, meeny, miny, moe," which is used to select a person during games. The person doing the picking starts the count saying some variation of "Eeny, meeny, miny, moe, / Catch a tiger by his toe. / If he hollers, let him go, / Eeny, meeny, miny, moe," pointing at a different participant each time they say a word of the rhyme. This method has proven good enough to choose roles in a game of tag, but it is an example of pseudorandomness, because there is an inherent structure to the rhyme. If you start with the same "seed"—in other words, start the rhyme pointing at the same person every time—you will always land on the same person at the end because the rhyme is inherently predictable, and thus not truly random.

Why would a Randonaut want to use pseudorandomness at all if it isn't truly random?

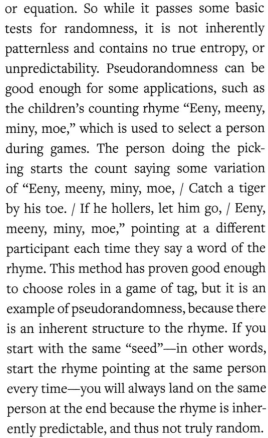

TERMS TO KNOW

Deterministic: in philosophy, determinism is the belief that all events, including human behaviors, are determined by previously existing external causes rather than human will. In mathematics, computer science, and physics, a deterministic system is one in which there is no randomness to affect the outcome of the system; therefore, a deterministic model will always produce the same result based on a particular starting condition.

Well, because it still helps you break determinism and get out of the stasis field. You see, if the mind-matter interaction hypothesis is correct, any random point you generate and influence with intention is entirely causal, or well within your current probability tunnel of possible choices. If you only ever went Randonauting using intention-based mind-machine interaction, you may never leave the stasis field at all, because you'd only go to points that you influenced. Using pseudorandomness is more likely to get you out of the stasis field.

Nondeterministic

The more raw entropy (unpredictability) an RNG has, the more powerful the possible mind-matter interaction effect. Processes that measure quantum fluctuations with high amounts of uncertainty offer a high degree of true entropy. Many sources of true randomness source their entropy from quantum processes, so when Randonauts refer to "quantum" random points, they are referring to random locations generated by a truly random quantum random number generator. "True" randomness is an event where the system containing the entropy lacks a causal trigger. Unlike pseudorandomness, this is about as random as you can get, and it's why we use this type of mechanism in Randonautica. Nondeterministic randomness contains more true entropy, making it useful for mind-matter interaction.

Trying to have an influence on matter (the world around you) isn't something unique to Randonautica. Other groups have experimented with RNGs to see if consciousness can interact with randomness to create patterns and order. In fact, Randonautica started by using the nondeterministic quantum random number generator (QRNG) located at Australian National University (ANU) in Australia.

TERMS TO KNOW

Quantum random number generator (QRNG): the equipment or process used for generating perfectly unpredictable random numbers, derived from a quantum source.

The university explains how their QRNG operates as follows:

"The random numbers are generated in real time in our lab by measuring the quantum fluctuations of the vacuum. The vacuum is described very differently in the quantum physics and classical physics. In classical physics, a vacuum is considered as a space that is empty of matter or photons. Quantum physics however says that that same space resembles a sea of virtual particles appearing and disappearing all the time. This is because the vacuum still possesses a zero-point energy. Consequently, the electromagnetic field of the vacuum exhibits random fluctuations in phase and amplitude at all frequencies. By carefully measuring these fluctuations, we are able to generate ultra-high bandwidth random numbers."

Though this QRNG was a great source for Randonautica, the app's creators couldn't use it for long. In early January 2020 Australia was overcome by widespread brush fires. This caused ANU to be closed and the QRNG to be unusable. Randonautica's early decentralized developer team moved quickly to create independent sources of randomness. After think-tanking several ideas, Randonautica began using a camera random number generator (CamRNG) developed by mind-machine interaction researcher Andika Wasisto. This CamRNG generates randomness using thermal fluctuations in a phone's camera sensor and an open-source library.

Mind-Matter Connections

An effort of human intention producing an effect on a mechanical process is called "psychokinesis," something commonly depicted in fantasy and sci-fi movies as a spectacular superpower. We are now learning that it might not be as rare as the movies make it seem and that with repeated, consistent practice, anyone may be able to develop these unique mental capabilities. When Randonauts deal with nondeterministic randomness (like lottery balls), we hypothesize that it allows for thoughts to have more influence on matter. At the heart and soul of Randonautica is the mind-matter interaction algorithm called Newton Library, which anyone can access through Randonautica's application programming interface (API), software that permits two applications to talk to each other. Newton Library is closed source, but it is accessible to use by anyone in Randonautica, so you can't see the code, but you can use it in Randonautica. The reason Randonautica harnesses true, nondeterministic randomness is because of this algorithm. The process is an example of a "majority vote" algorithm, where statistical anomalies are measured (remember, an anomaly is something that doesn't seem right). What does that mean? Newton Library sets thousands of random points all around a radius of your geographic location. Wherever those random points cluster to an improbable degree, we can hypothesize that an anomaly may reveal an interesting geographic location. By consciously intending to influence the random number distribution, you have aided the probability of finding whatever you are looking for. That's why you use a nondeterministic number source—one that can spit out different results every time.

Not every anomaly scan will yield something—sometimes there are simply no anomalies present. If there isn't a statistically improbable cluster of random points, no anomaly will be found. But there have been so many interesting stories of mind-bending experiences in which people have found things relating to what they were thinking or feeling or talking about when they were generating the point, that it sort of scratches the "existential curiosity itch" that any good aspiring mad scientist encounters. If you can visualize your consciousness influencing an RNG, and understand that you think and something happens, you are ready to start experimenting with randomness.

Global Consciousness and RNGs

Global consciousness, sometimes referred to as "field consciousness" or "the collective consciousness," is the notion that there is an invisible matrix that links all human beings. A significant group currently studying this idea is the Global Consciousness Project, which started as a parapsychology experiment in 1998. As described on their website:

> "The Global Consciousness Project is an international, multidisciplinary collaboration of scientists and engineers. We collect data continuously from a global network of physical random number generators located in up to 70 host sites around the world at any given time. The data are transmitted to a central archive which now contains more than 15 years of random data in parallel sequences of synchronized 200-bit trials generated every second.
>
> "When human consciousness becomes coherent, the behavior of random systems may change. Random number generators (RNGs) based on quantum tunneling produce completely unpredictable sequences of zeroes and ones. But when a great event synchronizes the feelings of millions of people, our network of RNGs becomes subtly structured. We calculate one in a trillion odds that the effect is due to chance. The evidence suggests an emerging noosphere or the unifying field of consciousness described by sages in all cultures."

The Global Consciousness Project also studies the ability of consciousness to influence RNGs. At a very basic level, they study the connection between minds and intentions, and the distribution of random data they've collected from devices. The project's experiments have pointed toward the possibility that human consciousness interacts with RNG devices at the quantum physical level. Specifically, one set of experiments found that when they put an RNG at a location where groups of humans were at a high level of coherence, like at an opera where a large number of people were listening to the same music and feeling the same emotions, the devices deviated from the expected normal distribution of random numbers. These experiments were known as "FieldREG," because they put random event generators (REGs), which are synonymous with RNGs, in the field. The results of the FieldREG experiments suggested that when people gathered together are on the same vibe or wavelength, the resonant energy produced will create unexpected effects on the RNGs.

Interestingly, when they placed RNGs in busy shopping malls or places that lacked the resonant coherence of a group, they found the RNGs did not deviate significantly from the normal expected outcome. The hypothesis they were testing was that consciousness produces the intelligent field (also called the "conscious field" or "information field") that we discussed in the previous chapter. They theorized that this conscious field may organize information that is absorbed by the random number sequence and cause it to create a trend that exceeds the boundaries of what is likely for a truly random process. The FieldREG experiments are considered by many to be a success, having a larger effect size than what they found in the sterile laboratory setting.

The researchers at the Global Consciousness Project went on to create a network of RNGs across the globe, referred to as the "EGG" (which stands for ElectroGaiaGram), that would pick up on large-scale events that seemed to affect the global intelligent field. Events such as the terrorist attacks on September 11, 2001, showed high levels of coherence among the RNGs of the EGG. These events drastically affected human consciousness and seemed to have a measurable effect on the RNGs, causing them to output data that was less random than expected.

The Global Consciousness Project also tests a theory they called "decision augmentation," which hypothesized that the mind could tap in to this intelligent field and know the results of an experiment before it happened. Could human beings be capable of reaching into the future and changing the present? That was one explanation. However, there is another hypothesis that human consciousness is capable of interacting with the physical world. The new age concept of "thoughts being things" is backed up by the theory of holographic reality, which supposes that our brains act as digital computers, encoding information using the left analytical brain to resonate with the right intuitive, instinctual brain in a binary process that produces a two-dimensional waveform, which is then projected into reality as a three-dimensional hologram. Similar to how pebbles are dropped into a still pool and cause ripples going outward, it is theorized that our minds are encoding information, which is then projected into reality.

History of Anomalous Research

People have been experimenting with the ability of the mind to influence matter for millennia. In fact, some of the most well-known scientific minds in history were interested in the phenomenon of the power of imagination changing outcomes. Isaac Newton, renowned for his theory of gravity, experimented with trying to influence dice rolls using the power of imagination. The field of parapsychology is the study of extraordinary human abilities, such as telepathy, psychic powers, and other paranormal phenomena. Research in this area is often described as anomalous, as it refers to data or situations that are outside of what you would expect to happen.

Helmut Schmidt's Research Into the Power of Our Minds

Many researchers have studied whether our minds can impact the world around us. Helmut Schmidt, a German-born physicist and parapsychologist, became very interested in RNGs while working at Boeing. He felt that sometimes RNGs weren't as random as they seemed, and theorized that the randomness seemed to correlate with his state of mind and intentions. In the 1970s, he created one of the very first mind-machine interaction experiments, a psychokinesis test that used electronic equipment. He used a string of lights and a QRNG to see if some of his subjective experiences could be validated. He asked experimenters to focus their intention on making the lights light up in a circle and tried to make them go clockwise or counterclockwise depending on their stated intent. He found statistically anomalous results—that is, people were able to influence the lights more frequently than the normal expected "random" outcome. Could there be some force or power behind the nature of consciousness that caused these random processes to behave not so randomly?

Intuition and Precognition

Have you ever had a sense that something was going to happen before it occurred? Or maybe you had a dream that ended up manifesting later in your life. Intuition and precognition, or the ability to sense an event will happen before it does, are topics of extreme importance to the field of parapsychology. Although the conclusions are widely contested, many scientists have studied in laboratory settings things most people generally find unbelievable, such as mind reading and healing people from faraway distances. Although there has historically been, and still exists, a taboo against using the scientific method to explore such things, there is a rich history of parapsychological studies dating back to the 1800s, when societies started using the scientific method to study anomalous phenomena during the rise of spiritualism and mediumship. Notable members of these groups included psychologists Carl Jung and Sigmund Freud.

Reading parapsychology studies can be incredibly captivating and exciting if you are interested in the possibilities of unique human capabilities. However, it can be hard to digest the findings portrayed in these studies if you aren't experienced generally in reading scientific papers and statistics. For instance, in the 1940s, parapsychologists began using the Greek letter Ψ (psi) as the variable for the potential psychic influence in a statistical anomaly. Obscure details like that can be hard to decipher at first, but don't let it discourage you if you have an interest, as parapsychology can be a very interesting and exciting field once you learn to discern some basic principles.

Feeling Someone's Gaze

Have you ever "felt" someone staring at you, and when you looked over they were indeed gazing at you? Although many may brush this off as mere coincidence, there have been parapsychology studies about this very thing. In a lab setting, studies (such as the ones conducted by Rupert Sheldrake) have found that some people really were able to sense when someone was gazing at them, and, even more interesting, when they added a shielding material in between the people, the effect could no longer be measured. This idea that someone's observation could actually make another person feel something may be challenging to some people's worldviews. Common knowledge says the observer doesn't *do* anything, so the observation is not causative. But given that some people can sense when a person's gaze is on them, and that using a physical material to shield the observer actually blocks the effect, how can we be so sure? Perhaps the reality is that consciousness influences matter in more ways than most people accept, or that things are connected more than we may know.

Remote Viewing

Remote viewing is the act of sensing information about an environment while unable to literally see it. Imagine someone gives you an envelope with a random number written on it and asks you to tell them what is inside the envelope without you looking in it. Completing that task would be an example of remote viewing. Experiments about and examples of remote viewing abound, although there is no prevailing theory on exactly how it works. For example:

- In 1973 (several years before a space probe visited the area), Ingo Swann, a famous remote viewer, said that he saw the rings around Jupiter.
- There are many released US government documents regarding the military's interest in these practices, such as programs like Stargate Project and the Gateway analysis and assessment.
- Remote viewing has been credited with solving crimes and locating missing people.
- Remote viewing techniques are routinely taught at conferences and seminars around the world.

When you use Randonautica, you are using a practical remote viewing application, where you set your intent to find something and receive information about a potentially interesting geographic location. The act of using Randonautica qualifies as remote viewing using anomalous cognition, gathering information you would not have had otherwise to find a personally meaningful or interesting location.

GOVERNMENT INTEREST IN REMOTE VIEWING

The US government officially conducted experiments in remote viewing as recently as 1995. The Stargate Project used anomalous cognition and remote viewing as ways of gathering operational intelligence.

There may be programs like this still in existence today that may be classified. Perhaps due to cultural reasons, the US did not openly research parapsychological phenomena as much as other countries (like Russia), where remote viewing and psychic experiments were more widely accepted. Nevertheless, the US military was interested in using anomalous cognition and remote viewing to gain actionable intelligence.

Correctly predicting probabilities of something happening is a valuable tool for those in power; for example, it can be used for:

- Gaining information about an enemy's location
- Economic gains, like predicting market movements

TERMS TO KNOW

Anomalous cognition: the practice of retrieving information from a distant point in space-time, the contents of which are typically blocked from our usual sensory systems by distance, shielding, or time.

Those in power throughout history have used scientific *and* divinatory means to predict the probabilities of something occurring. Just like the kings of old had augurs reading the movement of birds to tell them information about the future, those in power today are just as interested in predicting future probabilities. This puts the field of anomalous cognition squarely in the hands of a few power brokers, while the general public at large does not even have a good conception of the spectacular mental capabilities human beings are capable of possessing.

Mind-Matter versus Artificial Intelligence

One interesting thing about mind-matter interaction over other forms of predicting probabilities is that the human operator and its biofeedback are necessary for it to function. Artificial intelligence, on the other hand, can run on a computer without a human operating it. But unless actively training the skill of influencing material reality with your mind becomes a popular cultural phenomenon, it will lay in the hands of the few specialists who have spent years accumulating knowledge about this field. Part of the reason Randonautica exists is to wake people up to the possibility of mind-matter interaction, in the hopes of cultivating a cultural phenomenon where individuals are capable of influencing RNGs and other systems with their consciousness.

Princeton Engineering Anomalies Research (PEAR)

The Princeton Engineering Anomalies Research (PEAR) lab was started in the 1970s to study the effects of consciousness on random outputs, such as falling marbles, swinging pendulums, and fluctuations of mechanical quantum noise. The important thing to know about the research that happened at PEAR is that their statistical results deviated significantly from the normal results you would expect on the basis of scientific consensus. Brenda Dunne, the manager at the PEAR lab, was another one of these forward-thinking scientific minds who was not afraid to research outside of normal academic consensus.

The laboratory was based on play, and they would have groups of individuals come experiment with conscious intention and try to influence the random distribution of numbers on various systems, including microelectronic random event generators that used quantum effects, as well as macroscopic random systems, like a wall of nine thousand falling marbles on a maze of pegs, designed to represent statistical probability (they referred to this system as "Murphy").

PEAR got much of its funding because of the possibility that human consciousness could interfere with electronic systems. Robert Jahn, the head of PEAR, came from a background in aerospace and was concerned that the high intensity of psychological events in fighter pilot cockpits could possibly interfere with the electronic systems onboard. If a human operator could influence electronic systems thought to be secure, that represented a huge security risk.

However, there was a second, broader goal of understanding the role consciousness had in establishing reality. PEAR took subjective phenomena that had been reported for centuries and, for the first time, gave some credence through statistical evidence that human consciousness was capable of interfacing with systems. The researchers at the PEAR lab statistically analyzed experiments like the one that measured the influence a person had on a swinging pendulum, which would change colors based on the operator's intent. Their measurements were so fine-tuned that they were even able to measure the effect the nearby waves in the ocean were having on the pendulum! They found that the more the operator identified with the random device as an extension of themselves, the better the results. After thousands and thousands of trials, they would calculate by hand the statistical probability that their results were better than chance. The laboratory participants were anonymous, with no special claim to unique mental powers or capabilities.

The Princeton research was incredibly reassuring to many people who had subjectively experienced such phenomena but were met with resistance by the mainstream. The PEAR lab inspired generations of researchers to peek behind the veil and bravely challenge what was considered impossible. The researchers at PEAR found that the effect of consciousness influencing these random systems was not dependent on time or space:

- **Space:** Experimenters could affect the random distribution with their stated intentions if they were in the same room but also from far distances.
- **Time:** Participants found they could influence the randomness with intent, even if the random system didn't run until weeks later. People would sit down and attempt to influence an RNG that ran the next week, and they found results suggesting that this was possible—that intention could influence events throughout time.

One of the most interesting findings was that the RNGs seemed to cohere, or produce order out of randomness, when one or more random event generators were placed at gatherings of like-minded people. This finding seemed to suggest that people on the same wavelength or vibe could create an entangled energy that had a coherent effect on the random event generators. "Bonded pairs," or couples deeply in love and in tune with each other, had an even greater effect on the RNGs' cohering, a result that sort of mirrors the subjective experience of lovers experiencing telepathy.

CONNECTIONS BETWEEN PEAR AND RANDONAUTICA

The PEAR participants were invited to come to the lab and play in order to experiment with the effect of consciousness influencing randomness and probabilities. Randonautica draws on the same spirit of this group, with a focus on play, allowing people from all walks of life to experiment and have fun trying to influence randomness. These researchers were brave enough to challenge the mainstream academic consensus and use the scientific method to point to an ineffable mystery, which, although it has not yet been cracked, has a large body of statistical evidence pointing to its existence and usefulness. Randonautica took the two main parts of the

The Rubber Band Effect

Another discovery PEAR made that has been repeated in the Randonauts' research was the "rubber band" effect, where the operator would affect the RNG to an improbable degree, but to the opposite of their stated intention. This rubber band effect is something you will encounter as you train your anomalous psi abilities to influence RNGs and is a common experience you come across when learning the skill. This effect can skew results of an experiment, as the operator influences a distribution to an anomalous degree—but in the opposite of the intended direction, such as if you were trying to make a graph move up with your mind to an improbable degree, but instead it moved down.

PEAR laboratory research (operators influencing randomness and experiencing remote viewing) and created a synthesis that focuses on influencing probabilistic systems in search of meaning.

A lot of the discoveries made in the PEAR lab reflect the same anecdotes you find from Randonauts today, such as the "beginner's luck" effect. Researchers in the PEAR lab noted that first timers to influencing randomness would do extremely well on the tests, creating a large effect size that would point to a statistical anomaly, meaning it was likely that their consciousness influenced the distribution of randomness. But on the second or third try, the effect would diminish, until there was no statistical anomaly at all. The Randonauts eventually would go on to make the same discovery: When attempting to influence a random distribution and make a graph move up or down with your mind, there is a "beginner's luck" effect.

Randonaut Developers Try These Experiments

The core development team behind the Randonauts is not only interested in making mind-matter interaction technology accessible and easy to use for the public but also in experimenting with different variables in order to achieve an even greater effect size, or ability to measurably influence the distribution of randomness with consciousness. Becoming a skilled operator at influencing probabilistic systems includes several skills:

- A proficiency in meditation
- The ability to stay focused for an extended period of time
- Strong aptitude for visualization
- A lot of practice making graphs move up and down with one's mind (an operator will sit at a computer and attempt to focus conscious intention to make a line on a graph move up past a certain point that would indicate the possible existence of conscious influence)

Randonautica developers have friendly competitions to see who can influence the chart best, or even try to block another person from successfully beating chance and influencing the graph. There are other "psi games" that challenge the operator to successfully predict what color a square on the screen will turn.

YOU CAN TRY TOO!

Playing these games can help you develop the skill of influencing RNGs and is something any average person can begin doing with the right tools. You can try some of these games at www.randonautica .com. If you guess the correct color enough times over enough trials, you'll get real feedback as to just how much influence you hold over the random colors.

It doesn't take a great deal of mental strain to play these games—in fact, straining too much can give you a headache and cause your score to drop. The more you relax into the process and almost go into a trance, feeling the sequence of random data as an extension of yourself, the more success you will have. When you are able to consistently get a score greater than chance, you know you have trained yourself well. The Randonautica developers are generally able to correctly guess a binary decision 5 percent over chance, which would be like guessing a coin flip correctly fifty-five out of one hundred times.

Z-Score and Probabilities

As you have learned in this chapter, humans have the uncanny ability to influence randomness based on their stated intent. However, the actual amount of influence an individual can have is quite small—meaning, humans can only change the expected results by a small margin. This is why Randonautica makes use of a mind-machine interaction algorithm that amplifies the tiny bias consciousness creates on randomness. Scientists studying extraordinary and unique mental capabilities make use of statistics to see how these anomalies differ from the expected normal data. That's why if you go on to read journals about parapsychology and other consciousness studies, you will surely run into the concept of z-score.

Z-score tells you how many standard deviations you are from the mean. The higher the z-score, the farther it is from the normal, expected distribution. Z-score is used in Randonautica to show the likelihood that a certain point has been influenced by consciousness. Z-scores greater than 5 are considered interesting, because the deviation from the normal, expected outcome is so far outside of chance that the scientists studying Randonautica hypothesize the point has likely been influenced by the operator's conscious intent.

In the example of the Randonautica algorithm, which lays out thousands of random points and measures how densely they cluster, the z-score tells us how unlikely that cluster was to occur. If an attractor has a power of 5, that means it is five times more dense than the average amount of points on the map. The higher the score, the denser the cluster of random points, and the more likely that it has been influenced by intention.

The concept of "power level" also comes into play here. If you imagine the distribution of random points as forming hills and valleys, the power level gives you an idea of how high or low these valleys are, while the z-score represents volume (e.g., how many pounds of soil are in those hills).

Looking to the Future

What all these experiments and theories are shooting for is a bright future where you think, then something happens in the material world. There is no definitive theory of how mind-machine interaction is possible (most researchers suspect that it works via some form of quantum mechanics we haven't quite figured out yet)—which makes it all the more exciting to consider.

One of the ideas behind Randonautica is the feeling that it is everyone's responsibility to make sure that technologies that offer people access to the global conscious field remain public and accessible for anyone who wants to use them. Part of the technological revolution uniting consciousness with the material world depends on people developing amazing mental capabilities and becoming skilled operators at influencing randomness. It won't happen if this technology stays locked in a laboratory but only if there is a popular cultural change in how we use our minds to interact with systems.

A future where you walk into your house and the lights turn on because you *thought* that command will only be possible if people begin exploring mind-matter interaction technology for themselves. So, although making a graph move up and down on a computer screen with your mind may not seem very exciting, the implications of being able to responsibly use this technology for even greater applications in the future is something that motivates us and our fellow Randonauts!

WHAT YOU'VE LEARNED IN THIS CHAPTER

- Random number generators (RNGs) measure physical processes or properties that are truly unpredictable.

- Randomness isn't just "unexpected"; it is truly unpredictable.

- Deterministic randomness, or pseudorandomness, is randomness that looks random but was actually derived from a pattern.

- Nondeterministic, or true, randomness is truly unpredictable data derived from a quantum process.

- Randonautica uses pseudorandomness to help you get out of the stasis field.

- Randonautica uses true randomness for mind-machine interaction.

- The Global Consciousness Project tested the theory of a conscious field capable of ordering information in unstructured, random data.

- Parapsychology is the study of mental phenomena that are excluded by orthodox science.

- Remote viewing is the ability to sense information about a place while unable to literally see it.

- The Princeton Engineering Anomalies Research (PEAR) lab experimented with, and found some statistical evidence for, consciousness influencing electronic systems.

- Randonautica took the ideas of consciousness influencing electronic systems and the ability to sense a place remotely and applied them in the search for meaning.

- Influencing an RNG is a skill that can be honed, and there are tools you can use to become a skilled operator.

CHAPTER 5

Connecting to the World

One of the key issues many people face in pursuit of personal growth and development is the problem of a meaningless existence. One can often feel like a stranger in their own world, disconnected from reality and without a lifeline to an expressional, creative, and poetic perspective on their worldview. One of the main metaphysical arguments of Randonautica is that what you do matters: Your thoughts and your mind matter and have an effect on material reality. You are not disconnected from the whole; you are part and parcel of it.

This idea of universal consciousness, referred to by Carl Jung as *unus mundus*, means that the parts create the whole and that the network of sentient humans creates a global consciousness, which in turn creates consensus reality. The problem of a meaningless existence is solved once you realize that every decision you make matters and that life is a garden of forking paths that deserve careful consideration as you bravely travel new dimensions of consciousness. This inclination to connect with the holistic nature of the cosmos is not something new, and resonates in Randonautica as an echo reminiscent of the mystics of old.

Synchronicities and Meaningful Coincidences

Throughout history, humans have been fascinated by prophetic dreams and visions, in which people somehow imagine a future event. People have attributed prophetic dreams to several things:

- God and divinities at play in the world, not necessarily as miracles, but often as a wink and nod from the powers around us
- Simple coincidences arising from a meaningless random mental process
- Carl Jung's psychological view: synchronicity

Synchronistic phenomena go beyond dreams—they are meaningful coincidences, things that are truly out of the ordinary and without any conventional cause. Some common synchronicities are categorized as déjà vu (I've seen this before) and *déjà rêvé* (I've seen this in a dream), both of which have a distinct feeling that accompanies them.

When a Randonaut has a clear intention and then finds a corresponding object at their location, this is a prime example of synchronicity. Thus, both prophetic dreams and Randonautica-based discoveries share that amazing concept, synchronicity.

An easy way to grasp synchronicity is recognizing the connection between something internally known and something external and unknown. The seeming impossibility of these random connections is what makes their occurrence so striking. These events, if powerful enough, will stay with you and maybe even change your worldview.

Carl Jung's Concept of Synchronicity

The psychologist Carl Jung popularized the term "synchronicity" to categorize these bizarre but meaningful coincidences. They are called "synchronicities" because they synchronize the internal and external world, a meeting of the psyche with the material. While synchronicities are common occurrences in the course of therapy or in close relationships, as both individuals are "synchronized" to an almost (sometimes truly!) telepathic extent, Jung was interested in the random, seemingly impossible synchronistic phenomenon. He found it to be one of the strongest forces in his life, guiding him along his most important works.

He believed that synchronicities occurred through a "relativity" of the psyche, meaning that the unconscious mind experiences time and space in a way our conscious minds can't. So when a Randonaut experiences a synchronicity, it could be that they unconsciously perceived the future or distant space. Jung found that the unconscious mind was capable of perceiving beyond our senses, and that this unconscious, seemingly impossible sort of sixth sense was the root of all unexplained phenomena.

Jung thought there were three types of synchronistic phenomena:

1. Instant connections: when an internal state corresponds with something happening right now. This is also simultaneous phenomena.
2. Spatial: when an internal state corresponds with something happening far away.
3. Temporal: when an internal state corresponds with something happening a long time before or after the present.

To grasp all three, we need some clear examples.

INSTANT CONNECTIONS

Jung used a personal example for the instant connection phenomenon: A patient of his had a dream that she was given an expensive piece of jewelry, a golden scarab. While she described this dream to Jung, he heard a tapping at the window, and opened it to find a scarab beetle. He caught it, and handed it to the patient, saying,

"Here's your scarab." This astounded the patient and left a significant impression on Jung. Without any possible causal connection, a human discussion of a dream beetle coincided with the appearance of a real beetle. Randonauts engage in precisely these kinds of connections—random, impossible coincidences that arise in the pursuit of meaningful adventure.

SPATIAL SYNCHRONICITY

Spatial synchronicity explains the function of telepathy and ESP—essentially, ideas that the unconscious mind is able to see and hear farther than the eyes. The example Jung used was of the famous philosopher Emanuel Swedenborg, who had a distinct vision of a fire occurring in his home city of Stockholm while he was far away at a party—something that turned out to be true. His unconscious perceived the fire in a way that none of his other five senses possibly could have.

TEMPORAL SYNCHRONICITY

This type of synchronicity is one of the most fascinating, as it is the subject of many religions and magical practices. Temporal synchronicity describes the ability to see into the future or receive prophetic visions and dreams. These do, in fact, occur! As a Randonaut, you may be able to discern whether your meaningful experience was a product of ESP or a vision of a future yet to come. For example, you might have a dream or vision that foreshadows an event that later happens while Randonauting.

Synchronicity and Randonautica

In *Synchronicity: An Acausal Connecting Principle*, Jung writes, "The synchronistic factor merely stipulates the existence of an intellectually necessary principle which could be added as a fourth dimension to the recognized triad of space, time, and causality.... [U]nlike causality, which only allows us to draw conclusions from their logical precursors, synchronicity is a phenomenon that seems to be primarily connected with psychic conditions, that is to say with processes in the unconscious." He goes on to give an example:

"For instance, I walk with a woman patient in a wood. She tells me about the first dream in her life that had made an everlasting impression upon her. She had seen a spectral fox coming down the stairs in her parental home. At this moment a real fox comes out of the trees not 40 yards away and walks quietly on the path ahead of us for several minutes."

Jung's idea that synchronicity constitutes a fourth force in physics (along with space, time, and causality) is extremely significant to the Randonaut, as it places them outside the bounds of traditional causality! When a shocking synchronicity occurs on a journey, you can examine the synchronistic value rather than searching in vain for a nonexistent causal connection. As you do this, you free yourself from the conventional analytic instincts. Instead of thinking, *How did this get here?* or *How did this happen?* you can instead consider the *Why?* You can look for the symbolic, psychological, or emotional significance of the coincidence at hand. This is generally a far more fruitful and adept means of interacting with Randonautica.

Synchronicity As a Method of Divination

Divination can be seen as an example of synchronicity. Meaningful coincidences have long been the fascination of countless religions and philosophies, each trying to glean the significance of these improbable happenings. For example, ancient Chinese Taoists found synchronicity through a method of divination described in the *I Ching*. They would toss flower stalks or coins and find meaning in the positions they fell in. They interpreted the nature and character of that given moment through the construction of a hexagram made of six lines. The function of the *I Ching* divination rituals rested on the Tao, the universal energy, and its dual aspects—yin and yang—which represent how seemingly contrasting forces actually work together.

We see the same random synchronistic elements in some other divination methods, such as the tarot. Each of the seventy-eight cards in a tarot deck is given a unique symbolic value, and when shuffled, the outcome of various card pulls is entirely random. While some people aren't sure about the tarot's effectiveness, others find very clear synchronicities that arise from it! After all, there is no prior causal connection besides you shuffling the cards and picking one. Randonautica can be seen as a modern form of these divinatory technologies, all of which utilize symbolic understandings of random events to understand oneself and the world in a greater way.

Time Travel

Some Randonautica experiences are so far outside your own conception that the hair rises on the back of your neck and you question the very reality around you. One major topic of interest for the early researchers of Randonautica was that of time travel. After all, as Albert Einstein wrote, "For us believing physicists, the distinction between past, present and future is only a stubborn illusion."

Do We Need a Time Machine?
Popular entertainment, books, philosophers, and science fiction have hypothesized and visualized ways that an object or person might be able to move between different points in space and time. The prolific use of time machines in entertainment leads most people to believe in the idea that a device of some kind is how one object would be able to go from one time to another. However, when thinking of time travel as it relates to Randonautica, it's best to not

think of a special portal or teleportation device—the Randonautica car does not need to reach 88 miles per hour. Instead, the possibility that time travel (and other time-related theories like time distortion and time dilation—more on these concepts later in this chapter) exists might be due to the fact that everything, all matter and energy, is existing at once.

Imagining Time Travel via Tiny Particles

Even though you cannot see it, every particle in your body is connected to every particle in every other thing. Think of yourself as air, connected to all. In his book *Fractal Time*, Gregg Braden breaks down the concept of time as it relates to cycles and patterns into a timecode template, which Braden has determined through his personal research to include three apparent principles:

1. "The conditions of nature, including human events, do repeat themselves in cycles."
2. "The conditions of one cycle often repeat with a greater magnitude of expression in a later cycle."
3. "It's the return of the conditions, rather than the events themselves, that can be predicted."

As an example of this logic, let's take the April American tax deadline as an event. An adult in their forties has likely submitted their income tax returns on (or around) April 15 annually for a couple of decades. In the case where the majority of years the individual has had to pay money toward taxes, emotional feelings of dread, procrastination, and stress may accompany the tax preparation event. If this person's finances as they pertained to tax liabilities were to change one year, and they were expecting to receive a tax refund instead of owing, then the person should be relieved and filled with joy and excitement as tax day approached, right? In the theory of time as it pertains to cycles, whether an event presents a positive or negative outcome, the pattern will deliver a condition that repeats emotional resonance behind the ever-growing condition. Where in previous years the person would pay taxes in distress, they would now receive a substantial tax refund but have discovered that the roof on their home needs to be replaced, eating up the entire tax refund and causing the same feelings of distress and despair as felt in previous cycles.

The emotional resonance of the event sends tiny particles, like waves, flowing through the ether, packed with bits of information. The particles are not bound by space or time, so they can easily flow from past to future, future to present, so on and so forth.

By design, Randonautica uses chaos to influence pattern-driven outcomes. Because of the nature of quantum entropy, there is the possibility that engagement with this process of influencing probabilities connects your particles, especially those subatomic ones that make up your consciousness, to the world and people around you and opens access to the space-time field. These particles are given free reign and are not linked to a linear timeline. The particles seemingly create a vortex in which the individual may feel like time has stopped, sped up, or even become inconsistently distorted (i.e., the feeling of time moving very fast or slow or even standing still). Imagine entering a forest and checking your watch to see that the time is 2:34 p.m. You travel into the woods and get the feeling of having gone a great distance only to look back down at your watch and see that the time remains 2:34. It's almost as if time itself is an illusion, hmm?

Is it possible that the combination of breaking out of your stasis field; quantum entropy; and some highly vibrational human energy could be organic ingredients to achieve subtle time travel? If so, how would that be interpreted in theory and subjectively?

Possible Examples of Time Traveling in Randonautica

The subjective experience of the time-traveling Randonaut has many interpretations that are only truly understandable to the experiencer. The following perceived time-related phenomena have been reported while using Randonautica:

1. Reaching a void or attractor point and having the sensation that time no longer exists or has been distorted. For one user, everything was visually calm, and they experienced a sense of time moving very slowly. Later, they realized that what had felt like a few minutes had actually been an hour.
2. Going Randonauting, then returning to find significant things have changed. Some report that large objects like buildings were no longer in the same place, while others have less drastic observations, like small new items appearing with no explanation of where they came from, or noticing a product's brand logo is no longer the same.
3. Awakening in a new home or city without traveling and having a vague recall similar to déjà vu.

Of course, you could attribute these experiences to something other than time travel—such as false memories, dementia, or even lying or exaggerating. But for the sake of exploring new ideas, let's consider these experiences to be wholly real, without cognitive dissonance. How could these mind-boggling occurrences have happened?

In Example 1, the theory of time dilation can be used for speculation. You can think of time dilation as a sort of slowing down of time. The stronger the gravitational pull, the more space-time curves (if we think of it as a line), and the slower time itself proceeds. Perhaps, in some vibrational states, energy within the Randonaut can somehow build enough to push them out of their individual gravitational field, distorting time to the individual (and possibly also to others). None of this has been proven yet, but in the meantime, it's pretty trippy to think that a random location can warp how you perceive time.

In Example 2, the Mandela Effect is at play. This theory is used to explain when a large group of people realize they remember things differently than is generally known to be fact. The phenomenon was coined when a woman named Fiona Broome created a website in 2009 detailing her memories of Nelson Mandela's death in prison in the 1980s (though he was still alive at the time and did not die until 2013). Thousands of people flooded online forums with confusion, saying they remembered his death occurring in the 1980s too. This phenomenon is an example of what quantum theory is working to solve with the study of retrocausality. "Retrocausality" describes a phenomenon in which causality is reversed, meaning an effect can occur before its cause. Can the future affect the present, and can the present affect the past? Quantum entropy has retrocausal properties, and since Randonautica derives randomness through quantum entropy, it makes you wonder if all those particles breaking patterns are creating cause from the future!

In Example 3, things get complicated. Quantum teleportation has been researched heavily within academia as an important means for transmitting information in quantum computing. This concept is outside the scope of this book, but do your own research about it if it interests you. The bigger picture to think about is this: Is it possible that the human consciousness could use this same methodology to move about time? More curiously, are future Randonauts helping the existing Randonauts now? Did Randonautica open a gateway that diminishes the rigidity of the linear time concept? They are too complicated to explain here, but concepts like the quantum eraser experiment and the Asher Peres

TERMS TO KNOW

Retrocausality: also known as backward causation, a theory of cause and effect in which an effect can temporally precede its cause, and thus a later event can affect an earlier one.

paradox support the hypothesis that when you go Randonauting, an event in the future influences the past and causes you to observe an event at your random location. You can research these experiments further via a web search if you are interested in this topic (search on the topic "experimental delayed-choice entanglement swapping").

The team working on Randonautica has taken great care to ensure that our algorithm could demonstrate retrocausal effects. Although retrocausality is theoretical at this point, it's important to note that it has been considered to be a key to understanding time travel and even extreme space-time situations like traversable wormholes. It's fun to imagine that perhaps, just maybe, Randonautica has become a way to crack the door into what's yet to come for time travel. Maybe all Randonauts are time travelers, but the depth of the distance is limited...for now.

Other Unexplained Phenomena

It's not just time that gets wonky when you Randonaut. Other reports have shown that there might be some non-time-related, groundbreaking phenomena taking place that are yet to have reasonable explanations. These very real, often caught on camera occurrences have been reported by multiple people. Some of the strangest incidents include:

- **Electronics get glitchy.** For example, electronics in cars have ceased to work when nearing a void or attractor point.
- **People and animals are seen acting inexplicably oddly.** For instance, people have been seen staring frozenly or glaring out the windows of their homes at nothing. And a dog was seen standing, perfectly still, in the middle of the street, not moving for minutes (even blocking the Randonauts from getting to their point!).

- **Randonauts experience the long-lost friend phenomenon.** People have reported finding old friends or even family members at the exact location generated by the app. Videos of the genuine reactions of people recognizing one another in shock and confusion have baffled millions of viewers.
- **Observations related to intentions show up in uncannily specific ways.** For example, a woman who set out with the intention to find something that reminded her of her sister ended up finding a Bible in a parking lot with a message written on the inside of the front cover that included her sister's name and *exact* birthday.

These experiences pose another question that twists the Randonautica researcher's brain into a pretzel. Why do so many people seem to experience similar, extremely rare phenomena? Explanations involving memetics and global consciousness are a start to understanding, but imagine this: How baffled would you be to watch a video or read a Randonautica report that nearly exactly mirrored your experience? How about if you had a dream, and the next morning you woke up, checked *Reddit*, and saw that the bizarre dream you'd had was nearly identical to the top post in the Randonaut subreddit, and it was made while you were asleep! This type of phenomenon could have to do with Randonauts somehow accessing a hyperenclosed "quantum entanglement" system. Quantum entanglement is a physical phenomenon that occurs when multiple particles interact and become connected so that the state of one particle affects the others, even once they're separated. This phenomenon can even occur when the particles are not very close to each other.

How Can You Invite Unexplained Phenomena?

When creating your intent for a journey, if you wanted to see, for example, a red door, you'd set your intent to find a red door and vastly influence the probability of seeing a red door. But what if you wanted to find something so bizarre, you didn't even know what to look for? How do you set your intent to find things you never knew existed, also known as blind spots? To break out of the known and into the mystery, try setting your intent to:

- Learn something
- Discover something new
- Be surprised
- Be taken somewhere you have never gone before
- Experience hair-raising strangeness

Try these, or come up with your own intent that evokes some of the unexplained phenomena we've explored in this chapter.

The "Talking Walls" Effect

The "Talking Walls" effect describes the way that Randonauts see something at their location, often a mural or graffiti, that reflects something internal. This kind of symbolic synchronicity can be very significant and affirm the meaning of a Randonaut's journey. Talking

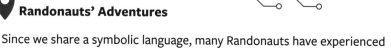

 Randonauts' Adventures

Since we share a symbolic language, many Randonauts have experienced symbols as part of their trips. A good example of talking walls was when someone found the names of their two cats engraved in the sidewalk. Another good example is when the popular *YouTube* livestreamer Ice Poseidon went Randonauting and found a baseball dugout that had a list of players tacked up in it. The list not only included his first name, but next to his name was the position he played in baseball when he was a kid. These kinds of one-in-a-million coincidences are commonly reported by Randonauts and scratch the existential itch of the curious reality explorer.

THE OFFICIAL GUIDE TO RANDONAUTICA

walls can feel like the universe is reaching out to speak to you in its own way.

Talking Walls As Pareidolia

Talking walls can be viewed as an artifact of "pareidolia," which describes when an observer sees meaning in abstract patterns, like seeing faces in trees or animals in clouds. Pareidolia is a natural tendency for humans and is an example of how people create significance in the absence of meaning. Something as simple as a few lines scribbled on a wall can come alive with meaning when you engage your imagination.

Children are naturally gifted at finding meaning and significance in abstract patterns that many grownups would not notice. That skill is often lost as people mature and are convinced that they ought not fill their heads with flights of fantasy, or else they may not fit in with society. But if you allow yourself to suspend your disbelief for a moment and engage with Randonautica as a game, which is a period of play, you can see the world through the lens of childlike wonder again, and simple abstract patterns can come alive with richness.

Owls: A Common Talking Wall Symbol for Randonauts

The wise and noble owl has been the mascot for Randonauts for a long time. They are one of the most prominent signs that

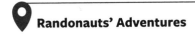

Randonauts' Adventures

One memorable trip report came from a relative who took a child Randonauting. The child set their intention for a "strange creature." On their journey, they came across a sign showing a quail crossing the street. The child, satisfied that the picture of the quail crossing the street fulfilled their intention, was so excited that they had gone out seeking a strange creature, and lo and behold they had found one! There is a lot to be learned from approaching the world with this kind of wonder and innocence.

Randonauts find while journeying. The owl has long symbolized wisdom due to its ability to see in the dark and its massive eyes. In history and myths, owls can be seen beside Athena, Ishtar, Ragana, and other great goddesses of wisdom. Similar to other divine birds, such as ravens and crows, owls symbolize a piercing intelligence. The Norse god Odin's two ravens (named Huginn and Muninn) would fly around the world each day gathering knowledge and bring it back for Odin to consider. Owls have functioned in a similar way for goddesses of wisdom: They see in the dark, gleaning and keeping secrets. Owls also announce change. They often show up around synchronous experiences and are commonly reported by people who experience strange and meaningful omens and coincidences. There are folk stories of people lost in the woods, dying of thirst, and when they see an owl, they end up following the owl as it leads them to water.

Many common cultural misunderstandings of the owl come from their kind of spooky appearance:

- Their heads rotate to an uncanny extent.
- They have great glaring eyes and huge claws.
- Their wings seem to flap silently.
- They tend to hoot loudly late in the night.

Some even believe owls to be the source of alien imagery and suggest that many alien sightings were, in fact, just people seeing owls.

Randonautica itself has been misunderstood in a similar way. Due to synchronicity being an essentially unconscious phenomenon, the repressed or unconscious parts of people can reveal themselves while Randonauting. But as with all ways of understanding darkness, the method is blamed. People assume Randonautica itself is picking creepy and negative locations, when in reality the users are given precisely what their intention is. In truth, owls are the perfect symbol of the Randonaut's experience: They go out into the unknown in search of things with a wide-eyed curiosity.

Finding the Guide

Randonauts aren't just limited to observing images on their adventures—they can also find people who contribute to their experiences in some way. While it's important to stay safe when Randonauting, finding the courage to interact with strangers is a great virtue: Countless Randonauts find that their journeys are not limited to places and things but also include people they must communicate with.

While adventures are often solo pursuits, the "heroes" of countless stories tend to come across other people who aid them. This is one of the major structural elements in the archetypal "hero's journey."

In many stories, when the hero is at the beginning of their venture, they find a wise guide to help them along their treacherous path, usually an elder. A few examples of this archetype are figures like Merlin, who guides King Arthur, or Obi-Wan Kenobi and Yoda, who help guide Luke Skywalker. They will often give the adventurer an important gift, whether it be a weapon like a light saber or Excalibur, or a valuable secret, like one's true destiny. While the people you meet Randonauting may not give you these literal gifts, there is a great deal to be gained from random, synchronistic interactions! Randonauts find that through their intentions, they end up at the right place at the right time and meet people who help them on their way. This is the beauty of synchronicity—when we go forth on an adventure, meaningful, powerful, and natural patterns arise from the randomness and bring us along our path.

Finding your guide can also take the form of looking within and trusting your intuition—in other words, you're your own guide. In Randonauting, that means that by feeling and sensing your inner state while traveling to unknown locations, you can find wisdom and learn valuable things about yourself.

You are the ultimate judge of something's meaning or significance. In this sense, finding the guide means looking inside for an answer, rather than relying on outside validation. Too often the first inclination someone has when seeking an answer is to look toward an external source, like googling the meaning of a symbol. Randonautica urges you to look inside for the answer, and only after you have first considered the meaning for yourself, go on to compare that answer with an external source.

The Pantheon

Beyond the guide, there are countless other figures from stories and myths who make themselves known to Randonauts. Carl Jung described these types of manifestations as "archetypes," or symbolic forms repeating throughout time in progressive guises. He viewed archetypes as the base for synchronicity, and as a kind of wavelength that connects the personal psyche to the outside. When Randonauts begin experiencing synchronicity, they are apt to be engaging with archetypal patterns or symbols, such as owls, black cats, rabbits, and so on.

These archetypal figures are understood through symbolism. But how do you pay attention to your adventures and their symbolism? You may have an intention of a certain figure, say, an owl, and at your location you may find an owl feather or nest. That's a pretty clear example, but symbols can be vaguer. Record the potential links between your intention and the outcome, even if they seem far-fetched. Thinking this way will make the obvious and objective coincidences far more powerful. If you find certain intentions reap fascinating and meaningful locations, keep digging!

When a Randonaut is able to understand and apply symbolic thinking, amazing synchronicities start to occur, as if "they" know that you are paying attention. This is similar to dreams: If you don't pay attention to your dreams, they won't have anything to say unless it's an emergency—but if you take time to record and consider your dreams, you foster a relationship with your unconscious, and you'll start to dream more frequently and clearly. When you record your Randonautica adventures (as you'll do in Part 2 of this book), you make it clear that they matter, and in doing so you open your potential for more meaningful adventures!

Memetics: A Consciously Connected Collective

The word "meme" has transformed greatly over time, just as memes themselves evolve. Evolutionary biologist Richard Dawkins coined the term "meme" in 1976 as a play on the Greek root *mim* (as in "mime" or "mimic") and the word "gene"—his concept was that of an idea or behavior that spreads and evolves (a "mental gene" of sorts) through cultural mimicking. He believed that memes are present in animals as well as humans, who learn and spread behaviors. The meme concept quickly made its way into esoteric philosophies, as it gave a scientific name to concepts that had long been understood and applied. Perhaps the most important evolution of the meme came around 1998, however, when the phrase was applied to Internet jokes. These Internet memes were really a perfect cognate for the evolutionary concept, because you could literally witness the evolution of Internet memes over a very brief period, and gain insight into the nature of the human mind.

What Makes Randonaut Memes Special

Like the parapsychological research that has produced Randonautica, the psychology of memes has been generally ignored and disregarded. Randonautica provides a suitable environment for those who study memetics, as one can see the mass spread of a given idea or symbol throughout countless Randonauts' experiences. Even more interesting is that now that Randonautica has gone international, the ideas transmitted virally by Randonauts are unlike those that spring up in any other way. Randonautica unites people from all walks of life, from all places around the globe, to tell their stories and find commonality.

Memes As Archetypes

Chris Gabriel, who runs the *YouTube* channel MemeAnalysis, views memes as a product of Carl Jung's archetypes. Just as archetypes produce symbols and symbolic experiences, memes are a modern understanding of this innate, synchronistic phenomenon. They play an important role to the psyche and spread important, powerful information through an invisible means. So while Randonauting, if you have a symbolic experience, you may be in the midst of a self-propagating meme (or idea) making itself known and spreading throughout your local area, the Randonaut community, the Internet, or even the world!

TERMS TO KNOW

Meme: a cultural or behavioral system that is passed from one member of society to another by nongenetic means, particularly by imitation. The study of memes is **memetics**. For the purposes of this book, the word "meme" is *not* being used to describe Internet photos.

What can memes tell us about the collective psyche? If we read memes as archetypal expressions, it follows that Randonauts share, to some extent, a collective unconscious, built up of these shared forms, ideas, and behaviors. When we analyze these communal memes, we can learn a great deal about ourselves. If you can learn to "read" memes just like you can "read" Randonauting experiences, you will get major insights into what's going on in the world. Because memes are transmitted virally, you can get a taste of what the collective unconscious is expressing by picking up on what sentiments are trending.

The memes that emerge through Randonautica represent a global mythos based around curiosity. Although synchronicity is extremely personal and strikes to the very core of who you are, it turns out it can be a shared experience. People from around the globe often report the same synchronous experiences, which in turn are shared as memes, and turn into legends if they become popular enough. These legends are folktales that arise through curiously exploring the void and emerge through the collective unconscious.

Memes versus Genes

Genes are typically thought of in a physical and biological sense. Memes, on the other hand, are more abstract and symbolic. One way to understand memes is through William S. Burroughs's concept of the "word virus." Burroughs was a prominent Beat author in the 1950s who was deeply fascinated by magic, the occult, and the potential of fringe science. Through his studies of the occult and psychology, he developed a concept called the word virus that was very similar to Dawkins's later meme. Burroughs viewed language itself as an autonomous organism, which spread itself like a virus does, infecting hosts, taking over, and continuing to spread. He grasped that certain powerful words held a great deal of unconscious power and could even affect people physically.

Finding Significance in the Mundane

Memes, like other products of the unconscious mind (such as dreams and fantasies) are consistently disregarded as meaningless. This is a defense mechanism, as we are very often frightened of what might be revealed about ourselves from these silly little things. And that's precisely the joy of Randonautica: It allows the user to look into the world around them with new eyes. In our mundane, day-to-day lives, we often lose sight of the beauty and mystery of our surroundings. When we use Randonautica, we are consistently brought face-to-face with new and mysterious places that are close by! What a bizarre experience, to see new things revealed about things we thought we knew like the back of our hands.

When Randonauting, we learn how much significance lies dormant, waiting to be seen right in our hometowns and stomping grounds. So many of the fascinating synchronicities that arise in the course of the journeys aren't taking place in strange and distant lands but directly in our own backyards. Randonautica invites users right into the heart of their land. The strange things we find in these spaces are certainly a cause for curiosity, as they carry a great mystery, a story we can never know. When you go to a big-box store and buy a product, it has the same story as every other item there, but when you Randonaut, it's like going to a thrift shop, full of interesting old items with fascinating stories behind them.

Randonauting brings users into a sort of romantic state of mind, where the world is enchanted again, and space is no longer just emptiness and a few places, but is full of meaning and invisible paths. This sort of romantic adventuring is a perfect cure for the apparent meaninglessness that infects so much of modernity. Randonautica is a promise that our home soil is still fertile, that beautiful things are growing now, and that wonderful things are still waiting to blossom.

Collective Storytelling Requires Patience

When magnificent coincidences arise naturally in the course of your experiences using Randonautica, they begin to compound, synchronicities pile up, and like a spread of tarot cards, they begin to resemble a story. When you see similar tales being spun across the community, it may well be that a legend is being born—a story that resonates across the collective, a meaningful form. Randonautica enables users to experience these stories and legends firsthand. While so many other apps and games serve as a way to make us comfortable while remaining physically and mentally inactive, Randonautica functions almost like an augmented reality, which invites users to directly interact with and investigate the world around them!

The world is enchanted by the telling of stories. They bring a glamour and shine to life, they give values and ideas to the communities that hear them, they make us feel things. So often, when we mature past youth, it feels as if life is no longer a journey, that our story has become dull and repetitive, and so many alternatives are sought out as a way to make life more enjoyable. Video games give you a story that you can live in virtually, and movies and TV shows act as places you can escape to. Randonautica is the antithesis of this type of escapism. It pulls you right into the reality of your environment and puts you face-to-face with the magnificence of the world.

While the stories we engage in are not always happy ones, they are all meaningful. They show us what we need and what we truly will ourselves to see. Many Randonauts may feel disappointed when a string of locations brings nothing of interest, but this is simply a part of the journey! When we watch movies and hear legends, the boring parts aren't included, but without them the stories never could have happened. So when you are just brought to a house or a yard, simply enjoy the ride! You are on the path to future curiosities, and there's no use in rushing. We get there when we get there. The story is being told both to and through us, and it is up to each Randonaut to record and share their experiences. We are collectively telling the story of Randonautica itself, our story. Each Randonaut is an adventurer and storyteller, so be sure to share your experiences and contribute to the legend!

This aspect that Randonautica brings of re-enchanting the world is special because the temporary suspension of disbelief and sincerity that comes with searching for strange things and synchronicities simply does not exist for most people in the throes of modern life. Too often are we expected to act "normal" and not engage with our intuition or inner lives in order to avoid seeming out of touch with society. Randonautica gives an opportunity for myths, legends, and symbols to come alive and a chance for you to experience a transformation of self seen through the lens of the hero's journey. Each random point you visit is an adventure into the unknown with the possibility for strange epiphanies and knowledge.

How We Respond to Uncertainty: The Randonautica "Despair Meme"

One of the most surprising phenomena associated with Randonautica is that of the "despair meme." The term uses *meme* to mean "a virally transmissible idea." The despair meme is the visceral physiological reaction some people have at the prospect of going to a random place, or even a fear of uncertainty in general. Since that random place is totally disconnected from any prior events in your life, your brain is attempting to predict what will happen when you get there. This response to uncertainty can cause some people to feel fear or anxiety, even manifesting as a projection of their worst fears. Sometimes at the mere prospect of going to an unknown location, people start to feel nauseated and sick or dizzy.

If the idea of visiting a Randonautica point is terrifying to you, for no apparently good reason, know that you're not alone. Although the despair meme is not evident in most people's journeys, it is a common enough phenomenon that it warrants the interest of the Randonautica developers. If even the mere prospect of going to an unknown location terrifies us, what other opportunities or possible decisions are we missing because of an unreasonable fear?

The despair meme is what makes the Randonaut's initiation into randomness such a thrill ride into the unknown—not just anyone is up to the challenge. By breaking through this barrier and seeing what is on the other side, you challenge your preconceived notions about what happens when you adventure into uncertainty.

Finding What You Look For

Scanning for anomalies is the same thing as scanning for a threat. When we're looking for something out of place, often our survival instincts will default to looking for dangerous things that threaten our well-being. It is no surprise that when encountering an unknown location, people often fear what they will find there. If you remember the discussions of intuition and law of attraction from earlier in this book, then you understand how when you look for something you are afraid of, you will often find it. Try to reframe this point of view, as the universe works in mysterious ways and will often repay you in kind. If you approach something with love and curiosity, you will be repaid in love and curiosity. But if you let your attention waver and give in to fear and despair, often that is what you will find. Energy follows intent, so keep that in mind when Randonauting. You will most likely find what you seek.

The Antidote to Despair

One of the prime directives of the Randonauts is to find the cure to despair. Despair creates an inertness in our daily lives, throwing up obstacles and impeding decision-making. The antidote is courage. Bravely facing your fears of uncertainty tells your brain that you are not afraid of going to an unknown place, and that those fears and anxieties you had are no longer needed. The survival response that tells you to be wary of new places and situations is a good thing—as it is ultimately there to protect you from real danger—so thank it for its service. But if your survival response runs rampant and finds danger where there is none, it can inhibit your development and make it hard for you to branch out and experience new paths in life.

By facing your fears and increasing your vantage point on holistic reality, you actually change how your brain works by creating new neural pathways. When you visit a random location that your brain and body are anxious about, you promote your ability to face uncertainty in everyday situations. In fact, "experiential diversity" has been scientifically proven to be good for your well-being. In a 2020 paper written in the journal *Nature Neuroscience*, researchers found that "daily variability in physical location was associated with increased positive affect in humans."

Is Hope an Antidote for Despair?

Are there any other antidotes for despair? Well, hope could be one. Instead of assuming there is some crazed ax murderer hiding in the woods you're being sent to—which paralyzes you with fear and keeps you from going to that strange random point in the middle of the woods—you could instead be optimistic and see the opportunity as a chance to involve yourself in novelty by exploring an unknown place. But hope is passive, and it is not a powerful enough emotion to truly overcome despair. Courage, however, is active. By putting courage into action, you are bravely challenging yourself to overcome the powerful feeling of despair that can keep you trapped inside your probability tunnel.

Using Courage to Maximize Your Randonauting Experience

Reframing your mind to feel brave is vital to becoming an avid Randonaut. What if, while you were out Randonauting, you found a being from a peripheral dimension? Would you run away, or would you approach it and attempt to learn something amazing from it? Of course, there have not been any reports of Randonauts finding beings from peripheral dimensions yet—but at a certain point, if there are enough people Randonauting, the odds of finding anything at all in existence become 100 percent.

What Makes You *You*? Exploring Identity with Randonautica

"Geography of thought" is the idea, developed by social psychologist Richard Nisbett, that where you were raised actually affects how your brain works. He observed that when shown the same photo, depending on where a participant was from, their eyes would gravitate toward different parts of the photo. Someone raised in the West would not focus on the same parts of the photograph as someone from East Asia. It turns out that where you were raised affects not only what possibilities you have been exposed to but also how your brain works at a fundamental level. If someone was raised on an entirely different planet than Earth but came here through a portal or a spaceship, you may be able to objectively prove that person was an alien because their eye movements when choosing what to focus on would be so different from anyone else's on the planet.

So much of a person's identity is based on where they were born; who they grew up around; and the thoughts, feelings, and experiences of those around them. But being a fully developed human is not just making the most of the hand you were dealt; it's challenging yourself to change your stars and explore degrees of freedom outside of the complex web of causality you were born within. Randonautica offers a route to explore self-development outside of the constraints of the mathematical patterns that limit your potential choices within the field of possibilities. Things like where you were born and the people you grew up around are no longer limiting factors in your ability to grow and change. Once you are able to explore new potentials and possibilities, you can experience things you never previously would have been able to conceive of.

The Drive to Seek and the Void Meme

In order to find out something new about yourself or the world, you must have some drive inside to seek something you are missing.

Even if you only have a vague sense of what you want to find, that is better than apathetically walking around with no internal compass. This inner drive of curiosity that spurs you to look for hidden treasures is what the Randonauts call the "void meme." This term describes the ability of the mind to create connections outside of any prior causal links. When a Randonaut goes to an unknown point, their brain is trying to predict what will happen next, so they create order out of the void in the form of a narrative.

Randonautica journeys can introduce you to this phenomenon, which can become a huge part of your personal growth. Oftentimes people report amazing synchronous experiences that changed their lives and their perspectives to such a point that Randonautica was a vital part of their self-development. This foray into the Genesis Field (a new web of probabilities that is found after escaping stasis) can allow you to develop intentionally into the kind of person you would like to be and help you to form new behaviors.

WHAT YOU'VE LEARNED IN THIS CHAPTER

- Synchronicity, or a meaningful coincidence, is a concept popularized by Carl Jung and is the principal thing Randonauts search for.

- Randonautica can help you experience iterations of time travel.

- Randonauts have mind-bending experiences that can often make people question if human minds are actually inherently separate from the matter around us.

- A "Talking Walls" effect is commonly experienced by Randonauts, and it can feel as if the universe is reaching out to speak to you personally.

- The owl represents wisdom. They see in the dark, and as Randonauts identify blind spots in their perceptual awareness, they become like the owl.

- Randonauting helps you trust your intuition and listen to that little voice inside or gut feeling. This process is also referred to as "finding your guide."

- Memes are ideas that spread virally. Within Randonautica, memes form a global mythos based around curiosity.

- "Despair meme" is a way to describe a common survival response to uncertainty. However, if this response is let out of control, it can be paralyzing and limiting to one's growth.

- The antidote to despair is courage.

- By increasing novelty and diversity in your experiences, you can literally change your brain to better handle adversity and uncertainty.

- Every Randonautica journey is the start of a story, and these stories can influence your self-development and help you on your hero's journey to becoming legendary.

CHAPTER 6

Getting Started

You've learned a lot so far! With all the knowledge you've gained on the historical, theoretical, and spiritual angles of Randonautica, you're primed for a successful start to accessing a fresh future for yourself by becoming a Randonaut. In this chapter, you'll become familiar with the final elements you need to set you on your new path. You'll learn how to journey safely, how to ground yourself before beginning, and the nine core tenets of Randonauting. This chapter will also help guide veteran Randonauts on how to advance their skill.

Being a Safe and Well-Prepared Randonaut

Before you begin your journeys, let's discuss the matter of safety as it pertains to Randonautica. First, be prepared for anything by doing these things:

- **Charge your phone:** If you need GPS to get you to your location, you're probably going to need it to get back as well. Randonauting can be mesmerizing, and it's easy to get caught up in going from point to point, but keep an eye on that battery level. Bring a car and/or portable charger as backup just in case.
- **Stay hydrated and nourished:** Until you've Randonauted, you won't know how your energy levels will react to the

experience. Some people have adrenaline pumping the whole trip. They report sweating and being light-headed simply because their brain is so amped for the excitement of the uncertainty. Other people find themselves trekking farther distances than expected, not realizing what a long way back they have until they turn around. Your adventure may have levels of exploration that require physical endurance, so pack snacks, water, and whatever else you need to stay nourished, and make sure you are taking care of yourself.

- **Consider going with a group:** There is no official stance on whether Randonauting alone or in a group makes for a better trip. It depends on the person and what type of experience you are going for. However, in terms of safety, if you are not normally comfortable walking or driving into an unfamiliar location by yourself, try to go with a friend or group. It can certainly make the experience more enjoyable, and there is safety in numbers. (Plus, you'll have more eyes to notice interesting things!)

Let's look at some more ways to stay safe on your adventures.

Introducing Friends to Randomness

It can be fun to take someone along who has never been Randonauting, but be aware it can be a disorienting experience for newcomers, sometimes even manifesting in physiological discomfort. Some anxiety from venturing outside of your normal routine and visiting unknown locations is normal. It is important to go at your own pace, and if someone in your group is experiencing some anxiety or disorientation from visiting random locations, take a moment to relax and take in the environment, and assure them that it is a normal survival response from being confronted with an uncertain situation.

Situational Awareness

Randonauting pushes you to open your mind and eyes to your surroundings. While doing that, you should follow some important practices to be mindful of your safety and surroundings. Here are ways to practice situational awareness while Randonauting:

- **Avoid trips at night.** Randonauts challenge their conscious ability to "see in the dark"—but not the *literal* dark. Going to an unknown terrain and area in the dark can reduce your situational awareness and make your trip less effective (in that you have limited observation because of the lack of light). On top of that, venturing into areas in the dark is not the safest choice and should be avoided.
- **Be respectful of private property.** In order for points to be truly random, the algorithm can't remove private properties, because, well, then it wouldn't be random.
- **Always look for "no trespassing" signs.** Even large, wooded areas can be private. An "abandoned" property might be a rundown family farm that's not being tended to, but it's still private. These areas could potentially contain hazards like sinkholes or other dangers, so it is not recommended to venture into large wooded areas without an experienced guide. In short: Never, ever, *ever* trespass.

Randonauts' Adventures

A woman was Randonauting and came across a house with multiple signs saying "welcome." She figured, *If they are so welcoming, why not knock on the door?* A man answered, and she explained that she had been sent to a random place using a quantum random number generator, and that it had sent her to his house. Wide-eyed, the man explained that he had been sitting down trying to write a speech he had to perform, and he had been experiencing writer's block. Right before the Randonaut had knocked on his door, he had asked for a sign from the universe.

- **Keep your mind open to good possibilities.** Perhaps you are a social person and feel safe in the neighborhood. In that case, you might consider knocking on the door and seeing if the person is home. Use your best judgment.
- **Get something out of the trip.** You can observe a house, a street block, numbers, things in a yard, etc. without trespassing. If you believe you were brought to a location for a reason, you probably were. Make the most of it. A point on a private property is not a lost trip.
- **Bring a garbage bag.** Sometimes Randonauting can make you feel out of place because you're visiting a new area. Picking up litter can make you feel more purposeful and secure.

Dealing with Unsafe and Dangerous Locations

The simple act of going to an unknown location brings thrill and excitement. Keep your adrenaline under control and don't take risks by trying to access areas that are clearly (or even have the remote possibility of being) dangerous. Train tracks, power facilities, and industrial complexes are absolutely forbidden. There are endless

Water Points

Often people who live in areas surrounded by water tend to have points that land in unobtainable parts of lakes, rivers, oceans, etc. Unless you plan to scuba dive or take out a boat, don't enter a body of water to reach a point. Sometimes the journey is just as important, if not more important, than the destination (as you learned in Chapter 3 of how a water point turned into an epic legend in Josh's giants' skeletons story).

adventures to be had, so there is no need to put yourself in a bad position.

Randonauting is about journeying into places that are unknown to you. Where you explore and exactly how close you get to a point might change as your level of comfort grows. Also, remember that there is always the possibility that maybe you weren't meant to take that journey or find that intention today. Trust your intuition and generate new coordinates if needed.

Grounding Yourself

Now that you've learned of the key safety aspects having to do with the physical world of Randonauting, you are ready to know some precautions in mental, emotional, and even spiritual preparations for using the app.

Overcoming Fear

One of the earliest commonalities among the original Randonauts was the feeling of fear or despair when heading into an unknown location. Experiencing fear or unease about going on a Randonaut trip is a very normal initial feeling (so much so that the community deemed this sensation the despair meme, which you can read about in Chapter 5). It takes practice, but clearing your mind and setting a positive intention can create a feeling of safety and a more rewarding experience.

Grounding is a technique often utilized in yoga and meditation practices. The terminology symbolizes connection with the earth or the ground. The goal is to bring your conscious awareness into the present and feel connected with the energy of the planet itself. Some common ways to practice grounding include:

- Taking off your shoes and walking on wet grass
- Visualizing your excess negative energy being incorporated back into the earth
- Putting the tip of your tongue up against the soft palate of your mouth behind your top front teeth and tucking in your coccyx

Reintegration

Before you have ever experienced Randonauting, you are in your probability tunnel, so after you Randonaut, you need to practice reintegration. Reintegration is the process of absorbing your epiphanies and realizations, being able to validate them, and using them toward a goal.

Reintegration is one of the most important parts of Randonauting and one of the reasons that engaging in the community and sharing your experience with other Randonauts can be wildly helpful. Here are some ways you can reintegrate:

- Write down the events that happened in this journal.
- Talk about your experiences with other like-minded but honest people.
- Meditate on your new realizations.

Reintegrating will help you apply what you learned and help you avoid any unproductive reality tunnels you may encounter on your journey.

The 9 Tenets of the Randonauts

The 9 Tenets of the Randonauts capture the core principles of Randonautica. These tenets were created to highlight what is most important to the Randonautica community and ensure that whoever is using the app is doing it responsibly, safely, and with the right intentions. These are important to keep in mind each and every time you embark on a trip.

1. **See in the Dark: Randonauts show a dedication to exploring the uncertainty and blind spots of the world around us.** "Seeing in the dark" is a figurative way to explain how Randonauts open their hearts, minds, and energy to things otherwise unseen, hidden in plain sight.

2. **Venture with Mindfulness: Pay attention and practice safety and situational awareness.** Being present and wholly aware keeps you and others safe and amplifies the experience.

3. **Be Sincere: Show compassion and a willingness to understand yourself and the community.** You're part of a phenomenon. Reporting synchronicities and helping build a global mythos based on curiosity requires sincerity. Experiencing quantum synchronicities strikes to the very root of who you are as a person, and that can't be faked. At the end of the day, everyone is united by being a Randonaut and being within the community. Support and open-mindedness are attributes of a true Randonaut.

4. **Maintain a High-Vibes Intent: Be luminous in thought and strive to radiate a positive mindset.** In being part of a growing group whose members have an impactful influence on one another in the conscious field, keep your intentions positive and always follow the golden rule when setting intentions: Do unto others as you would do unto yourself.

5. **Value Inner Life: Show appreciation toward the self as the catalyst for an effect on the external environment.** Seeking to better yourself helps to grow and create a beautiful space for future Randonauts. Go inward and self-reflect after journeys.

6. **Bridge Culture Gaps: Share experiences to assist in understanding the beauty of shared global consciousness.** Participating in the conversation can be an empowering experience for all Randonauts. Learning that someone on the other side of the world is having the same mind-bending experience can create a unity that is both life changing and uncanny.

7. **Transform and Shift: Curiously test the theory of quantum randomization and the possibility to change your life path or shift into a new, improved space and time.** Using Randonautica to better your life is more than just a self-help method. It's a tool that enhances the human experience. Open yourself to the idea that other dimensions of consciousness and better versions of yourself are easily accessible.

8. **Bring a Trash Bag: Be respectful of the environment and always leave the place you traveled to better than what it was before.** Set the tone for what a Randonaut gives back to the environment, this glorious landscape accessible to all. Treat it with care, and you'll find your Randonaut adventures have even the most practical meaningful outcome.

9. **Embrace Synchronicity: Dive into randomness to find connections and meaning for both yourself and the community.** Use serendipitous occurrences to guide you on your path. As the memetic structure unfolds within the growing collective, step into the web of connections by reading, watching, and reviewing others' stories. Individually, find deeper meaning in the signs and symbols that appear to you. It's often the case that the best storyline is unfolding progressively on each journey.

Different Ways People Randonaut

There is no one way in particular to "play" Randonautica. You might find that you use it for one of these common reasons, or that you have your own ideas! Watching other people's experiences as well as testing out different methods can provide you with a wide range of Randonaut skills that you can apply to have more successful and meaningful adventures. The more you practice and find out what works for you, the better you become.

To Spice Up Routine

Some people use Randonautica simply to add novelty to their otherwise mundane routines. This could be spicing up a route for a dog walk, choosing a new area to find a restaurant to eat in, or even changing the streets you travel on your way in to work. Taking the same routes, not only in your car but by foot, on a regular basis will ultimately lower your environmental observation, as your mind knows it's seen the scene. Mixing things up by letting the app direct something as simple as your daily dog walk can invigorate an otherwise simplified lifestyle in an easy and refreshing way.

The Free-Flow Approach

"Free-flow" Randonauts venture around and near the point but do not aim to find the exact location. This type of Randonaut is more likely to choose their own way to the destination instead of using the precise GPS route. The free-flow method is great for people who are simply looking to "see what they can see" and not necessarily hunting down a particular, exact point.

The free-flow method can also be more of a generalized approach to the Randonaut experience. For example, you might have a point in a park area, but instead of focusing on that one point, you spend time exploring the entire park—the people, cars parked in the parking lot, signage, etc. It's a broader approach to observing the journey and is likely to have the outcome of a comprehensive take on the trip (e.g., setting out for "happiness" and seeing that everything around the park was full of joy, laughter, bright colors, etc.).

The Precision Pro Style

If you're looking for improbable specificity, the precision pro style might be the best method for you. A Randonaut focused on precision will get as close to a point as possible (without breaking rules). Their objective is to find the exact location of the coordinates. This Randonaut is most likely to report a finding within a very small circumference. Finding an item or having a meaningful coincidence occur on the exact point can provide a sense of being dumbfounded. For example, an intention set to "something with my name on it" leads the Randonaut to a parked car, and hanging on the rearview mirror is a necklace that says "Jessica," the Randonaut's name. The more precise the point, the more uncanny it seems when something related to the intention set is uncovered.

Be Your Own Spirit Guide

Other Randonauts use a be-your-own-spirit-guide strategy. These Randonauts set out for a trip with their intuition leading the way and are likely to veer off course by following their gut instincts, signs, or other observational directions that speak to them but take them away from the original destination. Exploring on and around the point and taking detours while on the way to your point is a perfectly acceptable way to use Randonautica!

Content Creators

One of the biggest influences on Randonautica's rapid growth has been the users who document their journeys on video. These stories challenge the viewer's idea of what's possible using the app, and many are inspired to go on Randonaut trips of their very own.

These content creators may embody many of the different "types" of Randonauts, from the ghost hunters to the spiritualists to the photographers looking for inspiration. Content that shares an individual's or group's Randonaut experience is sensational and garners followers, subscribers, and viewers from around the world. There have even been many content creators, on *YouTube* for instance, who set out to fake a story and ended up smack-dab in front of truly anomalous finds! Whether it's a bit of a stretch or a genuinely shocking uncovering made on video, people of all ages and backgrounds have become enthralled with watching the Randonautica phenomenon unfold across digital media, which leads to...

Voyeurs

Yes, even the people who do not physically go out to a generated coordinate are members of the Randonaut community. Many people who are "lurkers" or consumers of the mind-bending reports found online have come to experience similar synchronicities and serendipitous events just from absorbing Randonaut information.

Watching other people's experiences as well as testing out different methods can provide you with a wide range of Randonaut skills that you can apply to have more successful and meaningful adventures.

Going Deeper: Becoming a "Pro" Randonaut

Randonauting can simply be a favorite pastime—or it can be an activity that deepens your lifestyle and amplifies the driving force in who you are. Early Randonauts committed a lot of thought and effort into understanding how to strengthen the impact of a trip. Through trial and error, strong reporting, and a highly engaged early community, Randonauts were able to discover several methods for increasing skills.

Try "Chaining" Points

The first and most common method of "advancing" is by going from one quantum point to the next to form a chain. You can chain points easily—just generate a new point from each coordinate, creating a progression of coordinates to travel to. As you string together these locations, you are creating a tremendous improbability that where you end up would ever have been possible for you without the influence of Randonautica.

Chaining points also challenges the depth of conscious awareness, memory, and connecting meaning over many points. Some Randonauts who have chained together more than twenty points in a single outing have reported that their intention was emphasized in their surroundings and findings as if it were a story unfolding.

Keep in mind that this is an advanced technique. To get started, try a five-point chain one day, a seven-point chain another day, and gradually build to something like twenty points.

Enlarge Your Radius

The more random your coordinates, the better your experience typically is—and setting a larger radius will allow the app to take a broader look for a point with a higher anomaly. Though the drive might be longer, traveling to coordinates outside an area you are familiar with will increase the likelihood that you'll end up in an area that is entirely new to you. The less you know about an area, the more likely you are to have increased observation and heightened awareness.

Some pro Randonauts enjoy generating quantum coordinates in new cities when they are traveling. Other Randonauts have advanced this skill to the point that they can leave their plans play-it-by-ear, or play-it-by-Randonautica, rather! "Intention: Find a restaurant with a spicy dish I'll enjoy!"

Deepen Your Understanding

Taking Randonauting to the next level isn't always about quantity of trips; it's also about the quality and level of your understanding. In the same way you can only gain knowledge in a certain subject after having learned the previous material, Randonauting drives you to expand your consciousness, ways of thinking, and emotional and psychological responses. With time, you learn how to be more imaginative than before. Reflecting on trips and gaining confidence in how you interact with certain types of points and combinations for deriving your coordinates will significantly improve your skill of garnering the best feedback from the world around you. For instance, you can test blind spots (places outside your normal conscious awareness) versus an attractor, which could lead you to somewhere potentially interesting or personally significant or meaningful. See if there are differences within the two in what your trip takeaways are.

Master Setting Intentions

As you become comfortable with the process, you can hone in on mastering intention as an objective. New Randonauts tend to

Randonauts' Adventures

A voyeur once watched a video where a group of men were on a Randonaut trip and came across a miniature horse that had escaped its gate. The video went on to show these men calling the police, who then came and helped wrangle the frightened miniature horse back into the fenced area where it belonged. The next day, a redditor posted a story that they had seen the video and for the first time in their life, they'd encountered a miniature horse in their neighborhood! To be clear, this person was not headed to a point generated by the app. The redditor was shocked and said, "I can't believe I organically walked up to a mini horse being taken to a birthday party the day after I saw this video! What are the chances?!"

lean toward broad intentions, such as happiness, the color purple, something creepy, peace, money, etc. Once you've expanded your scope of possibilities, you'll be able to narrow your intentions to specificity. For instance, you might set out an intention with multiple desires:

"I intend to find something awe inspiring, in nature, easily accessible, and safe to venture into."

Or you can create a very targeted intention:

"My intention is to find something that has my husband's name on it."

Your intention is like a subtle internal compass that allows you to navigate while surfing waves of synchronicities. The sort of waking-meditative state you can achieve while Randonauting is similar to the notion of "flow." Flow states are like when skilled martial artists are able to defend against a large force with grace and ease, or when a circus artist does an incredible physical feat seemingly effortlessly.

When you set your intention toward something, you have greatly influenced the probability of that event being observed. You can practice honing your skill of intention by telling yourself you are going to start noticing mundane things in your life—for example, something simple like seeing a purple flower that day. Once you begin setting intentions, you start seeing opportunities and possibilities all over that you would have missed before, and you start noticing events that harmonize with your stated intent. As soon as you start noticing this feedback loop—where you think about something happening and soon go on to witness it—you know your consciousness is becoming more in tune with the matter around you.

KEEP AN EYE OUT FOR LATENT OR CONFLICTING INTENTIONS

The theory behind setting an intention is that thoughts are causative—the observer doesn't just observe but can also effect change. One thing to make sure to pay attention to as you become more advanced is your latent desires. Conflicting latent desires can make it harder for your intention to manifest.

A good exercise is to write down all of your desires and see if any of them conflict with one another. Sometimes you think you want something, but deep down you really don't. Part of setting a good intention is knowing what you want. You should be extremely brief and really think about the words you are using to formulate your intention. It doesn't hurt to start looking up the specific meaning of the words you are using in the dictionary.

PRACTICE VISUALIZATION

Visualization, or imagining a picture of your intent in your mind's eye, is a great skill to train. If you are not visually inclined, focus more on embodying the state or emotion or feeling you most associate with your intent. Call up that "thing" in your imagination and meditate on it for an extended time. For instance, if you want to manifest a chair, sit and visualize a chair. Imagine the way the wood feels and how it smells. Think about how it was constructed and the things that went into making it. Try to imagine how it would feel to be that chair. Visualization and embodying different states will help you improve your ability to project whatever outcome you prefer.

Another practical exercise that will help you master intention is to come up with a sign or symbol that represents your intention and meditate while picturing that symbol in your mind. Once you have made some progress doing that, try coming up with five or more intention symbols that you meditate on while imagining them in a sequence. You can think of these exercises as a way of entrenching your intentions deep inside your unconscious mind. If you are easily able to call up any of these imaginal states at will, you will effectively boost the signal you broadcast when it comes time to influence Randonautica's RNG.

REMEMBER THE CONCEPT OF Z-SCORE

In training your intention, you can start to challenge yourself by seeing what effect you had on the quantum process in its return of the computation of the statistical power. As you become a skilled Randonaut, you can test to see if you can produce a higher power level and z-score, creating a more anomalous outcome with the distribution of the random numbers. This will go a long way as you track your progress in the adventure log and see if the higher scores result in more impactful results.

GO APP-FREE

People have been wandering based on their unconscious for eons. Once you get good at using Randonautica, an interesting challenge is to go out into the world and attempt Randonauting without the assistance of the app. Going on a meditative random walk, only being guided by your intuition, is a great thing to add into your Randonautica adventures. Remember, the real power behind Randonautica is the human mind. Once you start being guided by intuition and listening to your inner voice, you can start to tap in to a global mind that is not limited by normal human conceptions such as time and space. You will begin to feel an inner "knowingness" that teaches you the rhythm and flow of the universe's states.

There are many other methods of Randonauting without an app, such as the *dérive*. When you go on a *dérive* (or random walk), you allow the landscape of the environment to draw you in as you explore the parts of reality you probably would have missed as you passed by in your daily routine. Instead of walking down a sidewalk or street, you may walk in a straight line across an entire town. Going off the

Record Your Dreams

When it comes to the subconscious mind, there is no better place to find answers than in dreams. You can begin recording your dreams as well as your Randonautica trips and see if you can find any parallels. Dream logging requires you to create the daily morning habit of writing your dreams down. People are typically foggy in the morning, so the goal is to increase dream recall. That means don't touch your phone, don't start thinking about the day; instead, make the first motion of the morning grabbing a pen and journaling as much as you can recall from your dreams. Then compare the symbolism you find in your dreams with the findings in this Randonautica journal, and you can see if there is any interesting analysis that can be drawn from the comparison. Once you get good at recalling your dreams, you can start setting your intentions while Randonauting to see something you saw in a dream, and in this way you'll effectively be able to bring your dreams to life.

beaten path like this allows you to peek behind the normal frame of reality most people experience in their day-to-day.

You can also use the signs and symbols you find on your random walk to guide you. For instance, if you see an address with a repeating number, like 333, you could take that as a message to take a turn three blocks ahead. The landscape is now your guide, and whatever messages you receive tell you how to get to where you are going.

Another way to go Randonauting without the need for an app is with dice. You can throw the dice to see how many blocks to walk, and decide which way to turn by choosing to turn left if the number on a die is odd, or right if the number is even.

The Importance of Trip Logging

Even the most strikingly absurd Randonaut trip can be forgotten over time. That's why new and experienced Randonauts alike have found that the details of the feeling, symbolism, and meaning can best be saved by trip logging. This method allows you to organize and look back over your many adventures, like a scrapbook does for photos. Journaling has many other benefits as well.

Themes Will Become Clearer

You'll likely find that describing your journeys in as much detail as possible can allow for overarching themes to gradually develop. For instance, you might discover an interest hovering in the background that becomes a major focus of your life. This web of synchronicities can be linked back together while you're reviewing your trip logs.

You Can Explore Your Subconscious

Trip logging is also a way to check in with your subconscious mind and see how it's playing a role in what you are perceiving *or* receiving from the external. While you might be setting conscious intentions and starting to see the progressive outcome, your subconscious is equally, if not more, powerful—and yet it is likely a personal blind spot for people who haven't done deep digging into their internal selves. Looking through trip logs, you can find standout patterns that don't seem to fit what you consciously set out for. Pay attention to this! It could be revealing a deeper desire or maybe even your true calling!

Journey Into a World You Never Knew Existed

Randonautica is an international community of people united around curiosity. The signs and symbols that have clustered in the Randonautica sphere are projections of the collective mind of everyone who has participated in going on random adventures. The stories created by Randonauts are alive and transforming every time another Randonaut has a synchronous experience that reverberates in significance.

Wherever your journey leads you, and whatever significance you may uncover, the span of consciousness spent Randonauting is truly outside of your previous experience, disconnected from any prior events that led you there. It is a chance to form new perspectives, a new point of view. It is the opportunity to unlock new potential choices and outcomes, to form new loops and behaviors. Whatever you find, as long as it is meaningful to you, it is significant.

WHAT YOU'VE LEARNED IN THIS CHAPTER

- Staying safe while Randonauting includes practicing situational awareness and personal responsibility. Don't go anywhere alone you don't feel safe, never trespass, and make sure your phone is charged.

- Grounding yourself and staying centered is an important part of Randonautica. Reach out to your friends or the community for advice if you are feeling off-center.

- The 9 Tenets of the Randonauts provide a basic set of values for Randonauts to consider.

- People use Randonautica in different ways—experiment and find out what works for you!

- Become a master of your intentions by staying focused and paying attention.

- Log your trips! Patterns that you would not notice at first may develop over time.

- Once you are good at using Randonautica, you can try using your intuition to go "off the beaten path" and try exploring places using only your mind and landscape to guide your journey.

- The true Randonaut experience is about authoring *your* story and the reality around you.

PART 2

THE ADVENTURE LOG

These journal pages provide a place where you can fill out information from your Randonautica journeys. Start with the logistics, such as the date of your trip, starting point, radius, and coordinates obtained and whether you selected an attractor, void, or neither. Don't forget to mention how you will travel to your coordinates, as the journey itself is part of the adventure! Next, note your intention for the trip. As you travel to your point, note anything you observe along the way. Describe the location itself once you arrive. After your trip, it's time to reflect. Are you noticing any patterns? What thoughts and feelings arose for you during this trip? Use these prompts as a way to heighten your sense of awareness and sharpen your observational skills.

Feel free to write down (or draw) anything that comes to mind. In fact, bring this book along with you on your journeys. What might seem like a mundane detail at the time may in fact happen each time you go Randonauting. Or better yet, it may be a pattern happening to other Randonauts as well. Remember, no detail is too small. As is the nature of Randonauting, your conscious awareness will grow as you open your mind to soak in everything you see, hear, and feel along the way.

Be prepared to embark on a journey that will open your awareness to an alternative view on how to interact with the reality around you!

DETAILS OF MY TRIP

DATE:

STARTING POINT:

RADIUS AROUND POINT:

COORDINATES:

ATTRACTOR: ☐ **VOID:** ☐ **NEITHER:** ☐

MODE OF TRANSPORTATION:

✚ MY INTENTION:

✚ OBSERVATIONS EN ROUTE TO POINT:

✚ DESCRIPTION OF THE POINT ITSELF:

+ PATTERNS I'VE NOTICED FROM PREVIOUS TRIPS, OR OTHER RANDONAUTS' TRIPS:

+ MY THOUGHTS AND FEELINGS BEFORE, DURING, AND/OR AFTER MY JOURNEY:

+ OTHER REFLECTIONS:

DETAILS OF MY TRIP

DATE:

STARTING POINT:

RADIUS AROUND POINT:

COORDINATES:

ATTRACTOR: ☐ **VOID:** ☐ **NEITHER:** ☐

MODE OF TRANSPORTATION:

+ MY INTENTION:

+ OBSERVATIONS EN ROUTE TO POINT:

+ DESCRIPTION OF THE POINT ITSELF:

+ PATTERNS I'VE NOTICED FROM PREVIOUS TRIPS, OR OTHER RANDONAUTS' TRIPS:

+ MY THOUGHTS AND FEELINGS BEFORE, DURING, AND/OR AFTER MY JOURNEY:

+ OTHER REFLECTIONS:

DETAILS OF MY TRIP

DATE:

STARTING POINT:

RADIUS AROUND POINT:

COORDINATES:

ATTRACTOR: ☐ **VOID:** ☐ **NEITHER:** ☐

MODE OF TRANSPORTATION:

+ MY INTENTION:

+ OBSERVATIONS EN ROUTE TO POINT:

+ DESCRIPTION OF THE POINT ITSELF:

+ PATTERNS I'VE NOTICED FROM PREVIOUS TRIPS, OR OTHER RANDONAUTS' TRIPS:

+ MY THOUGHTS AND FEELINGS BEFORE, DURING, AND/OR AFTER MY JOURNEY:

+ OTHER REFLECTIONS:

DETAILS OF MY TRIP

DATE:

STARTING POINT:

RADIUS AROUND POINT:

COORDINATES:

ATTRACTOR: ☐ **VOID:** ☐ **NEITHER:** ☐

MODE OF TRANSPORTATION:

✛ MY INTENTION:

✛ OBSERVATIONS EN ROUTE TO POINT: | **✛ DESCRIPTION OF THE POINT ITSELF:**

+ PATTERNS I'VE NOTICED FROM PREVIOUS TRIPS, OR OTHER RANDONAUTS' TRIPS:

+ MY THOUGHTS AND FEELINGS BEFORE, DURING, AND/OR AFTER MY JOURNEY:

+ OTHER REFLECTIONS:

DETAILS OF MY TRIP

DATE:

STARTING POINT:

RADIUS AROUND POINT:

COORDINATES:

ATTRACTOR: ☐ **VOID:** ☐ **NEITHER:** ☐

MODE OF TRANSPORTATION:

+ MY INTENTION:

+ OBSERVATIONS EN ROUTE TO POINT:

+ DESCRIPTION OF THE POINT ITSELF:

✚ **PATTERNS I'VE NOTICED FROM PREVIOUS TRIPS, OR OTHER RANDONAUTS' TRIPS:**

✚ **MY THOUGHTS AND FEELINGS BEFORE, DURING, AND/OR AFTER MY JOURNEY:**

✚ **OTHER REFLECTIONS:**

DETAILS OF MY TRIP

DATE:

STARTING POINT:

RADIUS AROUND POINT:

COORDINATES:

ATTRACTOR: ☐   **VOID:** ☐   **NEITHER:** ☐

MODE OF TRANSPORTATION:

✚ MY INTENTION:

✚ OBSERVATIONS EN ROUTE TO POINT:

✚ DESCRIPTION OF THE POINT ITSELF:

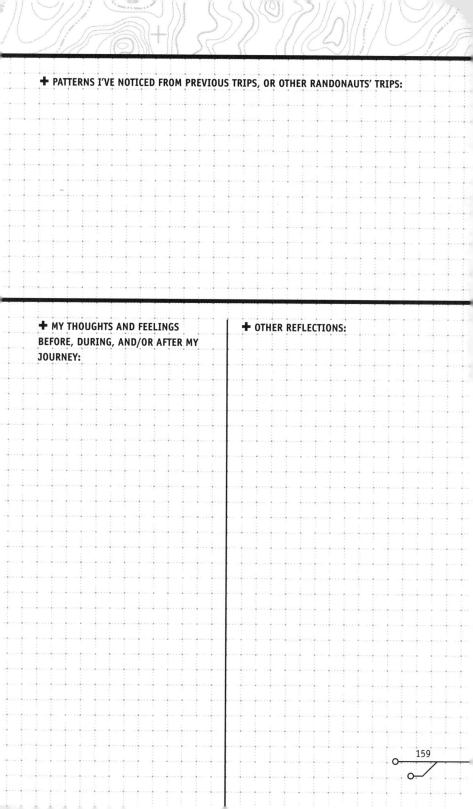

+ PATTERNS I'VE NOTICED FROM PREVIOUS TRIPS, OR OTHER RANDONAUTS' TRIPS:

+ MY THOUGHTS AND FEELINGS BEFORE, DURING, AND/OR AFTER MY JOURNEY:

+ OTHER REFLECTIONS:

DETAILS OF MY TRIP

DATE:

STARTING POINT:

RADIUS AROUND POINT:

COORDINATES:

ATTRACTOR: ☐ **VOID:** ☐ **NEITHER:** ☐

MODE OF TRANSPORTATION:

+ MY INTENTION:

+ OBSERVATIONS EN ROUTE TO POINT:

+ DESCRIPTION OF THE POINT ITSELF:

✚ PATTERNS I'VE NOTICED FROM PREVIOUS TRIPS, OR OTHER RANDONAUTS' TRIPS:

✚ MY THOUGHTS AND FEELINGS BEFORE, DURING, AND/OR AFTER MY JOURNEY:

✚ OTHER REFLECTIONS:

DETAILS OF MY TRIP

DATE:

STARTING POINT:

RADIUS AROUND POINT:

COORDINATES:

ATTRACTOR: ☐ **VOID:** ☐ **NEITHER:** ☐

MODE OF TRANSPORTATION:

+ MY INTENTION:

+ OBSERVATIONS EN ROUTE TO POINT:

+ DESCRIPTION OF THE POINT ITSELF:

+ PATTERNS I'VE NOTICED FROM PREVIOUS TRIPS, OR OTHER RANDONAUTS' TRIPS:

+ MY THOUGHTS AND FEELINGS BEFORE, DURING, AND/OR AFTER MY JOURNEY:

+ OTHER REFLECTIONS:

DETAILS OF MY TRIP

DATE:

STARTING POINT:

RADIUS AROUND POINT:

COORDINATES:

ATTRACTOR: ☐ **VOID:** ☐ **NEITHER:** ☐

MODE OF TRANSPORTATION:

+ MY INTENTION:

+ OBSERVATIONS EN ROUTE TO POINT:

+ DESCRIPTION OF THE POINT ITSELF:

+ PATTERNS I'VE NOTICED FROM PREVIOUS TRIPS, OR OTHER RANDONAUTS' TRIPS:

+ MY THOUGHTS AND FEELINGS BEFORE, DURING, AND/OR AFTER MY JOURNEY:

+ OTHER REFLECTIONS:

DETAILS OF MY TRIP

DATE:

STARTING POINT:

RADIUS AROUND POINT:

COORDINATES:

ATTRACTOR: ☐ **VOID:** ☐ **NEITHER:** ☐

MODE OF TRANSPORTATION:

+ MY INTENTION:

+ OBSERVATIONS EN ROUTE TO POINT:

+ DESCRIPTION OF THE POINT ITSELF:

✚ PATTERNS I'VE NOTICED FROM PREVIOUS TRIPS, OR OTHER RANDONAUTS' TRIPS:

✚ MY THOUGHTS AND FEELINGS BEFORE, DURING, AND/OR AFTER MY JOURNEY:

✚ OTHER REFLECTIONS:

DETAILS OF MY TRIP

DATE:

STARTING POINT:

RADIUS AROUND POINT:

COORDINATES:

ATTRACTOR: ☐　**VOID:** ☐　**NEITHER:** ☐

MODE OF TRANSPORTATION:

✚ MY INTENTION:

✚ OBSERVATIONS EN ROUTE TO POINT:

✚ DESCRIPTION OF THE POINT ITSELF:

+ PATTERNS I'VE NOTICED FROM PREVIOUS TRIPS, OR OTHER RANDONAUTS' TRIPS:

+ MY THOUGHTS AND FEELINGS BEFORE, DURING, AND/OR AFTER MY JOURNEY:

+ OTHER REFLECTIONS:

DETAILS OF MY TRIP

DATE:

STARTING POINT:

RADIUS AROUND POINT:

COORDINATES:

ATTRACTOR: ☐ **VOID:** ☐ **NEITHER:** ☐

MODE OF TRANSPORTATION:

+ MY INTENTION:

+ OBSERVATIONS EN ROUTE TO POINT:

+ DESCRIPTION OF THE POINT ITSELF:

+ PATTERNS I'VE NOTICED FROM PREVIOUS TRIPS, OR OTHER RANDONAUTS' TRIPS:

+ MY THOUGHTS AND FEELINGS BEFORE, DURING, AND/OR AFTER MY JOURNEY:

+ OTHER REFLECTIONS:

DETAILS OF MY TRIP

DATE:

STARTING POINT:

RADIUS AROUND POINT:

COORDINATES:

ATTRACTOR: ☐ VOID: ☐ NEITHER: ☐

MODE OF TRANSPORTATION:

+ MY INTENTION:

+ OBSERVATIONS EN ROUTE TO POINT:

+ DESCRIPTION OF THE POINT ITSELF:

✚ PATTERNS I'VE NOTICED FROM PREVIOUS TRIPS, OR OTHER RANDONAUTS' TRIPS:

✚ MY THOUGHTS AND FEELINGS BEFORE, DURING, AND/OR AFTER MY JOURNEY:

✚ OTHER REFLECTIONS:

DETAILS OF MY TRIP

DATE:

STARTING POINT:

RADIUS AROUND POINT:

COORDINATES:

ATTRACTOR: ☐ **VOID:** ☐ **NEITHER:** ☐

MODE OF TRANSPORTATION:

+ MY INTENTION:

+ OBSERVATIONS EN ROUTE TO POINT:

+ DESCRIPTION OF THE POINT ITSELF:

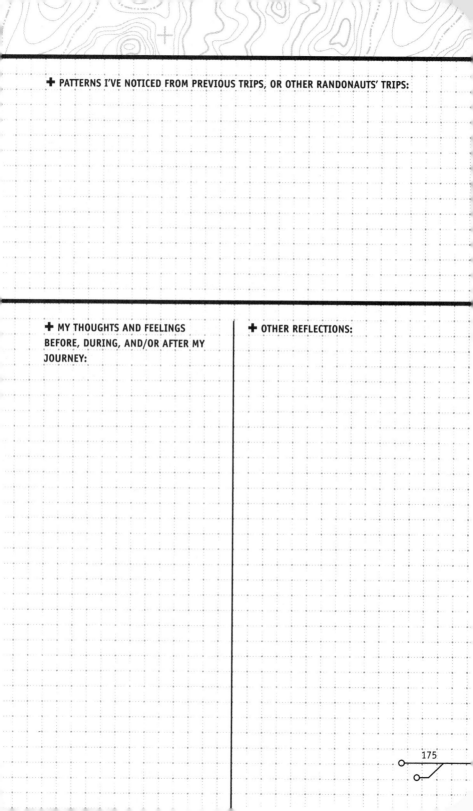

+ PATTERNS I'VE NOTICED FROM PREVIOUS TRIPS, OR OTHER RANDONAUTS' TRIPS:

+ MY THOUGHTS AND FEELINGS BEFORE, DURING, AND/OR AFTER MY JOURNEY:

+ OTHER REFLECTIONS:

DETAILS OF MY TRIP

DATE:

STARTING POINT:

RADIUS AROUND POINT:

COORDINATES:

ATTRACTOR: ☐ VOID: ☐ NEITHER: ☐

MODE OF TRANSPORTATION:

+ MY INTENTION:

+ OBSERVATIONS EN ROUTE TO POINT:

+ DESCRIPTION OF THE POINT ITSELF:

+ PATTERNS I'VE NOTICED FROM PREVIOUS TRIPS, OR OTHER RANDONAUTS' TRIPS:

+ MY THOUGHTS AND FEELINGS BEFORE, DURING, AND/OR AFTER MY JOURNEY:

+ OTHER REFLECTIONS:

DETAILS OF MY TRIP

DATE:

STARTING POINT:

RADIUS AROUND POINT:

COORDINATES:

ATTRACTOR: ☐ **VOID:** ☐ **NEITHER:** ☐

MODE OF TRANSPORTATION:

+ MY INTENTION:

+ OBSERVATIONS EN ROUTE TO POINT:

+ DESCRIPTION OF THE POINT ITSELF:

+ PATTERNS I'VE NOTICED FROM PREVIOUS TRIPS, OR OTHER RANDONAUTS' TRIPS:

+ MY THOUGHTS AND FEELINGS BEFORE, DURING, AND/OR AFTER MY JOURNEY:

+ OTHER REFLECTIONS:

DETAILS OF MY TRIP

DATE:

STARTING POINT:

RADIUS AROUND POINT:

COORDINATES:

ATTRACTOR: ☐ **VOID:** ☐ **NEITHER:** ☐

MODE OF TRANSPORTATION:

+ MY INTENTION:

+ OBSERVATIONS EN ROUTE TO POINT:

+ DESCRIPTION OF THE POINT ITSELF:

+ PATTERNS I'VE NOTICED FROM PREVIOUS TRIPS, OR OTHER RANDONAUTS' TRIPS:

+ MY THOUGHTS AND FEELINGS BEFORE, DURING, AND/OR AFTER MY JOURNEY:

+ OTHER REFLECTIONS:

DETAILS OF MY TRIP

DATE:

STARTING POINT:

RADIUS AROUND POINT:

COORDINATES:

ATTRACTOR: ☐ **VOID:** ☐ **NEITHER:** ☐

MODE OF TRANSPORTATION:

✚ MY INTENTION:

✚ OBSERVATIONS EN ROUTE TO POINT:

✚ DESCRIPTION OF THE POINT ITSELF:

+ PATTERNS I'VE NOTICED FROM PREVIOUS TRIPS, OR OTHER RANDONAUTS' TRIPS:

+ MY THOUGHTS AND FEELINGS BEFORE, DURING, AND/OR AFTER MY JOURNEY:

+ OTHER REFLECTIONS:

DETAILS OF MY TRIP

DATE:

STARTING POINT:

RADIUS AROUND POINT:

COORDINATES:

ATTRACTOR: ☐ **VOID:** ☐ **NEITHER:** ☐

MODE OF TRANSPORTATION:

➕ MY INTENTION:

➕ OBSERVATIONS EN ROUTE TO POINT:

➕ DESCRIPTION OF THE POINT ITSELF:

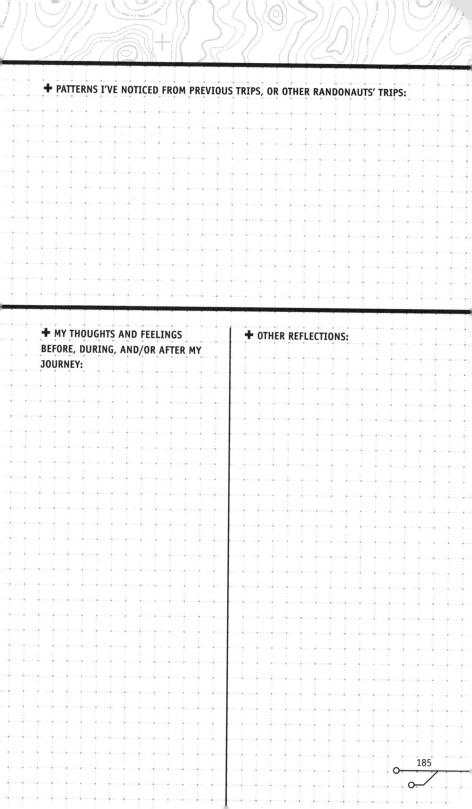

+ PATTERNS I'VE NOTICED FROM PREVIOUS TRIPS, OR OTHER RANDONAUTS' TRIPS:

+ MY THOUGHTS AND FEELINGS BEFORE, DURING, AND/OR AFTER MY JOURNEY:

+ OTHER REFLECTIONS:

DETAILS OF MY TRIP

DATE:

STARTING POINT:

RADIUS AROUND POINT:

COORDINATES:

ATTRACTOR: ☐ **VOID:** ☐ **NEITHER:** ☐

MODE OF TRANSPORTATION:

+ MY INTENTION:

+ OBSERVATIONS EN ROUTE TO POINT:

+ DESCRIPTION OF THE POINT ITSELF:

186

+ PATTERNS I'VE NOTICED FROM PREVIOUS TRIPS, OR OTHER RANDONAUTS' TRIPS:

+ MY THOUGHTS AND FEELINGS BEFORE, DURING, AND/OR AFTER MY JOURNEY:

+ OTHER REFLECTIONS:

DETAILS OF MY TRIP

DATE:

STARTING POINT:

RADIUS AROUND POINT:

COORDINATES:

ATTRACTOR: ☐ **VOID:** ☐ **NEITHER:** ☐

MODE OF TRANSPORTATION:

✚ MY INTENTION:

✚ OBSERVATIONS EN ROUTE TO POINT:

✚ DESCRIPTION OF THE POINT ITSELF:

+ PATTERNS I'VE NOTICED FROM PREVIOUS TRIPS, OR OTHER RANDONAUTS' TRIPS:

+ MY THOUGHTS AND FEELINGS BEFORE, DURING, AND/OR AFTER MY JOURNEY:

+ OTHER REFLECTIONS:

DETAILS OF MY TRIP

DATE:

STARTING POINT:

RADIUS AROUND POINT:

COORDINATES:

ATTRACTOR: ☐ **VOID:** ☐ **NEITHER:** ☐

MODE OF TRANSPORTATION:

✚ MY INTENTION:

✚ OBSERVATIONS EN ROUTE TO POINT:

✚ DESCRIPTION OF THE POINT ITSELF:

+ MY THOUGHTS AND FEELINGS BEFORE, DURING, AND/OR AFTER MY JOURNEY:

+ OTHER REFLECTIONS:

DETAILS OF MY TRIP

DATE:

STARTING POINT:

RADIUS AROUND POINT:

COORDINATES:

ATTRACTOR: ☐ **VOID:** ☐ **NEITHER:** ☐

MODE OF TRANSPORTATION:

✚ MY INTENTION:

✚ OBSERVATIONS EN ROUTE TO POINT:

✚ DESCRIPTION OF THE POINT ITSELF:

+ PATTERNS I'VE NOTICED FROM PREVIOUS TRIPS, OR OTHER RANDONAUTS' TRIPS:

+ MY THOUGHTS AND FEELINGS BEFORE, DURING, AND/OR AFTER MY JOURNEY:

+ OTHER REFLECTIONS:

DETAILS OF MY TRIP

DATE:

STARTING POINT:

RADIUS AROUND POINT:

COORDINATES:

ATTRACTOR: ☐ **VOID:** ☐ **NEITHER:** ☐

MODE OF TRANSPORTATION:

+ MY INTENTION:

+ OBSERVATIONS EN ROUTE TO POINT:

+ DESCRIPTION OF THE POINT ITSELF:

+ **PATTERNS I'VE NOTICED FROM PREVIOUS TRIPS, OR OTHER RANDONAUTS' TRIPS:**

+ **MY THOUGHTS AND FEELINGS BEFORE, DURING, AND/OR AFTER MY JOURNEY:**

+ **OTHER REFLECTIONS:**

DETAILS OF MY TRIP

DATE:

STARTING POINT:

RADIUS AROUND POINT:

COORDINATES:

ATTRACTOR: ☐ **VOID:** ☐ **NEITHER:** ☐

MODE OF TRANSPORTATION:

➕ MY INTENTION:

➕ OBSERVATIONS EN ROUTE TO POINT:

➕ DESCRIPTION OF THE POINT ITSELF:

+ PATTERNS I'VE NOTICED FROM PREVIOUS TRIPS, OR OTHER RANDONAUTS' TRIPS:

+ MY THOUGHTS AND FEELINGS BEFORE, DURING, AND/OR AFTER MY JOURNEY:

+ OTHER REFLECTIONS:

DETAILS OF MY TRIP

DATE:

STARTING POINT:

RADIUS AROUND POINT:

COORDINATES:

ATTRACTOR: ☐ **VOID:** ☐ **NEITHER:** ☐

MODE OF TRANSPORTATION:

+ MY INTENTION:

+ OBSERVATIONS EN ROUTE TO POINT:

+ DESCRIPTION OF THE POINT ITSELF:

+ PATTERNS I'VE NOTICED FROM PREVIOUS TRIPS, OR OTHER RANDONAUTS' TRIPS:

+ MY THOUGHTS AND FEELINGS BEFORE, DURING, AND/OR AFTER MY JOURNEY:

+ OTHER REFLECTIONS:

DETAILS OF MY TRIP

DATE:

STARTING POINT:

RADIUS AROUND POINT:

COORDINATES:

ATTRACTOR: ☐ **VOID:** ☐ **NEITHER:** ☐

MODE OF TRANSPORTATION:

+ MY INTENTION:

+ OBSERVATIONS EN ROUTE TO POINT:

+ DESCRIPTION OF THE POINT ITSELF:

+ PATTERNS I'VE NOTICED FROM PREVIOUS TRIPS, OR OTHER RANDONAUTS' TRIPS:

+ MY THOUGHTS AND FEELINGS BEFORE, DURING, AND/OR AFTER MY JOURNEY:

+ OTHER REFLECTIONS:

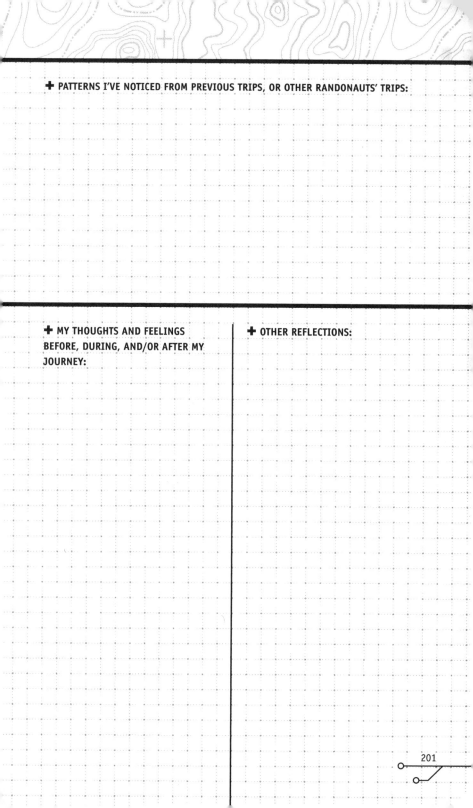

DETAILS OF MY TRIP

DATE:

STARTING POINT:

RADIUS AROUND POINT:

COORDINATES:

ATTRACTOR: ☐ **VOID:** ☐ **NEITHER:** ☐

MODE OF TRANSPORTATION:

✚ MY INTENTION:

✚ OBSERVATIONS EN ROUTE TO POINT:

✚ DESCRIPTION OF THE POINT ITSELF:

+ PATTERNS I'VE NOTICED FROM PREVIOUS TRIPS, OR OTHER RANDONAUTS' TRIPS:

+ MY THOUGHTS AND FEELINGS BEFORE, DURING, AND/OR AFTER MY JOURNEY:

+ OTHER REFLECTIONS:

DETAILS OF MY TRIP

DATE:

STARTING POINT:

RADIUS AROUND POINT:

COORDINATES:

ATTRACTOR: ☐ **VOID:** ☐ **NEITHER:** ☐

MODE OF TRANSPORTATION:

✚ MY INTENTION:

✚ OBSERVATIONS EN ROUTE TO POINT: **✚ DESCRIPTION OF THE POINT ITSELF:**

+ PATTERNS I'VE NOTICED FROM PREVIOUS TRIPS, OR OTHER RANDONAUTS' TRIPS:

+ MY THOUGHTS AND FEELINGS BEFORE, DURING, AND/OR AFTER MY JOURNEY:

+ OTHER REFLECTIONS:

DETAILS OF MY TRIP

DATE:

STARTING POINT:

RADIUS AROUND POINT:

COORDINATES:

ATTRACTOR: ☐ **VOID:** ☐ **NEITHER:** ☐

MODE OF TRANSPORTATION:

+ MY INTENTION:

+ OBSERVATIONS EN ROUTE TO POINT:

+ DESCRIPTION OF THE POINT ITSELF:

✛ MY THOUGHTS AND FEELINGS BEFORE, DURING, AND/OR AFTER MY JOURNEY:

✛ OTHER REFLECTIONS:

DETAILS OF MY TRIP

DATE:

STARTING POINT:

RADIUS AROUND POINT:

COORDINATES:

ATTRACTOR: ☐ **VOID:** ☐ **NEITHER:** ☐

MODE OF TRANSPORTATION:

+ MY INTENTION:

+ OBSERVATIONS EN ROUTE TO POINT: **+ DESCRIPTION OF THE POINT ITSELF:**

+ PATTERNS I'VE NOTICED FROM PREVIOUS TRIPS, OR OTHER RANDONAUTS' TRIPS:

+ MY THOUGHTS AND FEELINGS BEFORE, DURING, AND/OR AFTER MY JOURNEY:

+ OTHER REFLECTIONS:

DETAILS OF MY TRIP

DATE:

STARTING POINT:

RADIUS AROUND POINT:

COORDINATES:

ATTRACTOR: ☐ **VOID:** ☐ **NEITHER:** ☐

MODE OF TRANSPORTATION:

✚ **MY INTENTION:**

✚ **OBSERVATIONS EN ROUTE TO POINT:**

✚ **DESCRIPTION OF THE POINT ITSELF:**

+ PATTERNS I'VE NOTICED FROM PREVIOUS TRIPS, OR OTHER RANDONAUTS' TRIPS:

+ MY THOUGHTS AND FEELINGS
BEFORE, DURING, AND/OR AFTER MY
JOURNEY:

+ OTHER REFLECTIONS:

DETAILS OF MY TRIP

DATE:

STARTING POINT:

RADIUS AROUND POINT:

COORDINATES:

ATTRACTOR: ☐ **VOID:** ☐ **NEITHER:** ☐

MODE OF TRANSPORTATION:

+ MY INTENTION:

+ OBSERVATIONS EN ROUTE TO POINT:

+ DESCRIPTION OF THE POINT ITSELF:

+ PATTERNS I'VE NOTICED FROM PREVIOUS TRIPS, OR OTHER RANDONAUTS' TRIPS:

+ MY THOUGHTS AND FEELINGS BEFORE, DURING, AND/OR AFTER MY JOURNEY:

+ OTHER REFLECTIONS:

DETAILS OF MY TRIP

DATE:

STARTING POINT:

RADIUS AROUND POINT:

COORDINATES:

ATTRACTOR: ☐ **VOID:** ☐ **NEITHER:** ☐

MODE OF TRANSPORTATION:

✚ MY INTENTION:

✚ OBSERVATIONS EN ROUTE TO POINT:

✚ DESCRIPTION OF THE POINT ITSELF:

+ PATTERNS I'VE NOTICED FROM PREVIOUS TRIPS, OR OTHER RANDONAUTS' TRIPS:

+ MY THOUGHTS AND FEELINGS BEFORE, DURING, AND/OR AFTER MY JOURNEY:

+ OTHER REFLECTIONS:

DETAILS OF MY TRIP

DATE:

STARTING POINT:

RADIUS AROUND POINT:

COORDINATES:

ATTRACTOR: ☐ **VOID:** ☐ **NEITHER:** ☐

MODE OF TRANSPORTATION:

+ MY INTENTION:

+ OBSERVATIONS EN ROUTE TO POINT:

+ DESCRIPTION OF THE POINT ITSELF:

+ MY THOUGHTS AND FEELINGS BEFORE, DURING, AND/OR AFTER MY JOURNEY:

+ OTHER REFLECTIONS:

DETAILS OF MY TRIP

DATE:

STARTING POINT:

RADIUS AROUND POINT:

COORDINATES:

ATTRACTOR: ☐ **VOID:** ☐ **NEITHER:** ☐

MODE OF TRANSPORTATION:

+ MY INTENTION:

+ OBSERVATIONS EN ROUTE TO POINT:

+ DESCRIPTION OF THE POINT ITSELF:

+ PATTERNS I'VE NOTICED FROM PREVIOUS TRIPS, OR OTHER RANDONAUTS' TRIPS:

+ MY THOUGHTS AND FEELINGS BEFORE, DURING, AND/OR AFTER MY JOURNEY:

+ OTHER REFLECTIONS:

Glossary

Algorithm:

A set procedure to be followed for performing calculations or solving other problems, especially by a computer.

Anomalous cognition:

The practice of retrieving information from a distant point in space-time, the contents of which are typically blocked from our usual sensory systems by distance, shielding, or time.

Anomaly:

A deviation from the expected, normal order of things.

Deterministic:

In philosophy, determinism is the belief that all events, including human behaviors, are determined by previously existing external causes rather than human will. In mathematics, computer science, and physics, a deterministic system is one in which there is no randomness to affect the outcome of the system; therefore, a deterministic model will always produce the same result based on a particular starting condition.

Divination:

The practice of using supernatural methods to shed light on the future or the unknown.

Entropy:

In scientific terms, entropy is a measure of the amount of thermal energy per unit of temperature that cannot be converted into mechanical work, often interpreted as a measure of disorder or randomness in the system. In lay terms, it is a measure of randomness.

Holistic:

Relating to the understanding that the parts of a whole are intimately interconnected and inextricable from the whole.

Meme:

A cultural or behavioral system that is passed from one member of society to another by nongenetic means, particularly by imitation. The study of memes is **memetics**. For the purposes of this book, the word "meme" is *not* being used to describe Internet photos.

Mind-machine interaction:

The mind interacting specifically with machines or technology to demonstrate an influence on matter.

Mind-matter interaction (MMI):

A theory that consciousness and matter interact with each other in all forms, and particularly that intention can impact material reality.

Probability tunnel:

An abstract representation of the idea that limited decision-making possibilities based on a human's previous experiences and patterns create a likely "probable" response.

Quantum:

In physics, the smallest possible discrete unit of any physical entity involved in an interaction.

Quantum random number generator (QRNG):

The equipment or process used for generating perfectly unpredictable random numbers, derived from a quantum source.

Randomness:

Unpredictability; the quality or state of being without a pattern or framework of organization.

Retrocausality:

Also known as backward causation, a theory of cause and effect in which an effect can temporally precede its cause, and thus a later event can affect an earlier one.